CONFEDERATE WINTER

Kurt M Vetters With James R Knight

Copyright © 2015 Kurt M Vetters
All rights reserved.

ISBN: 1512113328
ISBN 13: 9781512113327
Library of Congress Control Number: 2015907589
CreateSpace Independent Publishing Platform
North Charleston, South Carolina

TABLE OF CONTENTS

Prologue vii
1. Trouble at Home 1
2. The Trouble with Work 7
3. Boy in Charge 12
4. The Newest Rebels 17
5. The Regiment 26
6. Off the Cliff 33
7. Big Plans 39
8. An Important Job! 43
9. On the Move 48
10. Across the River 52
11. Road March 56
12. Ashwood 63
13. The Elephant 69
14. Almost Home 86
15. Ready to Fight 93
16. Dying Like Men 99
17. Carnage 106
18. The Wounded 111
19. Regroup 116
20. Digging In 118
21. A Letter 123

22.	Yankee Attack	126
23.	Retreat	132
24.	Mattie	136
25.	Moonlight	140
26.	Shelter	143
27.	A Surprise	147
28.	Face to Face with the General	151
29.	Bushwhackers	156
30.	Home	159
Epilogue		163
Author's Note		165

DEDICATION

To my Father and all the parents that pass on the history gene on to their children.

PROLOGUE

Gray Riders

Young William Sweeney peered through the crack in the door at the five shadowy horsemen. The year of 1864 had brought many visitors to the Sweeney farm, none with good intentions. Hands sweating, William clutched the rifle his father had left him the year before.

The swirling fall mists of late October hid the identity of the riders. If they were mounted they were most certainly cavalrymen, and William had long since stopped caring if they wore blue or gray. He knew they were after the food and shelter the farm offered, and William's job was to do his level best to keep them from taking everything.

The riders approached without a sound. By this time in the war, riders had learned to be silent. All the buckles and straps that two years ago jangled away were carefully wrapped in rags and padded to stifle any noise. Only the breathing of the horses and the steady clop of their hooves gave their approach away. The riders pulled their horses up to the farm's disheveled gate and dismounted among some small trees.

"Hello the house," one rider yelled as the morning haze blurred his form.

"We're armed in here," William called back, "but you can water at the well and I'll put some food out for you on the porch. We ain't got much but you're welcome to what we can spare. Send one man up when I say and I'll pass some biscuits out."

"William, it's me, Mr. Ambers," the rider called back. "We need to talk to you, son. I'm walking up now, so don't you get careless with that peashooter of yours. I've only got one good arm left and I'd like to keep it intact."

Mr. Ambers came from town. He, like so many others, had gone off to war as a young man in 1861, and had come back old and broken a year and a half later. He survived the big battles at Shiloh and Murfreesboro, but it had taken him more than a year to ride again. Since so many of the local men were dead or off fighting, Mr. Ambers acted as the unofficial constable in the county. His personal crusade was to help his neighbors and kin survive the war. He had become indispensable to many of the small farms that lay scattered in this rolling hill country, serving as postmaster and the bearer of the horrible news of lost loved ones.

William's father, John, had been pulled into this deadly conflict last year, after the Rebel army had been chased down to Chattanooga. Yankee riders came through the county, drafting men and horses to take the fight deep into Georgia. Since Pa left fifteen months ago, William and his Ma, sister and brother had heard nothing. The lack of knowledge was a painful burden for his mother, so William was forced to become the man of the house very quickly and now, at fourteen, was in charge of the farm and all the mouths it had to feed. William got angry every time he thought about his father off fighting in the war, living the great adventure, while he was stuck here tending the hard and unforgiving farm. How could his father have put him in this awful situation?

"Come on up, Mr. Ambers," William called out, "but come alone and tell me who you got there with you." The additional riders made William nervous. In these hard times more than one man on horseback had to mean trouble of some kind.

Mr. Ambers spoke briefly to the men accompanying him and then leaned down and pulled the leather strap off the gate. Dismounting, he walked his horse to the Sweeney cabin. The other riders held their horses outside the rail fence. William watched one of the men refasten the lock. Probably another farmer, William thought, with a respect for people's property and the habit of closing up things. William appreciated that.

As Mr. Ambers approached, William's sister Becky came out of the cellar followed closely by their little brother Jim. Jim was 10 and tried to be a help to William around the farm, but he was small and mostly got in the way. The toy rifle William had carved for him was shaking in his hands, but he wore a look of determination. Ma followed them out. Fear gripped her and tears streamed down her face as she held a wooden spoon in front of her like a dough-covered cross. William winced when he saw the expression of terror on her face at the sound of footsteps approaching. Ma had been like this since Pa left, and William knew it was once again up to him to save this situation. Well, he thought, I don't need Pa. I can take care of this like I always do.

Mr. Ambers slowly tied his reins to the post outside the door and looked around the farmyard in one long, rotating gaze.

"You're place needs some work, William. Your Pa's counting on you to keep the fences mended and the wood stacked. I don't see any chickens or hogs around, so either you've been cleaned out or you have them hidden off in the woods." Mr. Ambers stepped up on the porch and addressed the still closed door.

"Pa's off playing soldier, Mr. Ambers. He's off having fun while I'm stuck here taking care of all this. Who you got with you today," William asked through the door. "Anyone we should worry about?"

"That's a fair question, William. Seems like trouble always comes on horseback. Foraging parties, bummers, deserters, and wayward soldiers are about all we ever see around here. Folks like you and me can't afford to be off our property much anymore, what with all these scalawags roaming around."

"But I'm here to talk to you about what's coming and your new part in it. I'd like to do it man to man, not through this front door. The riders with me seem to be pretty decent fellows. They're Alabama men, riding for the South. Seems like this war is about to touch us again in a big way, and that's why we're here. I think your family will be safe around these fellows, but they're a mite hungry."

William turned and gave his Ma a stern look and she nodded, sweat glistening on her brow. He leaned his back against the door. William took a deep breath and exhaled slowly, a habit he had unconsciously learned from his father. Anytime big decisions had to be made, Pa had a habit of stopping and taking a long, deep breath. It was a quirk of personality William hated, and he tried to fight the fact that he had inherited it. He thought you should act first and ask questions later. That was how a real man should go through life, and William thought of himself as a grown man.

Stepping back and mustering his courage, he opened the door and walked outside.

"Becky, get some biscuits ready for these men while I talk to Mr. Ambers," he called back over his shoulder as he strode out onto the porch, closing the door behind him. Mr. Ambers noticed the adolescent crack in his voice.

Cradling his rifle in the crook of his arm, he reached for Mr. Ambers' outstretched good arm, his left.

"Let's sit on the stoop, Mr. Ambers, while Becky gets some grub for you and the riders. If it's all right by you, I'll send the food out to them with Jim so we can talk."

"That's fine, William, but we need to speak quickly. Those men are on a recruiting visit," he said, gesturing toward the gate, "and you know what that means. They plan to take you and me with them, and any other able-bodied men they can locate this week.

Seems General Hood has moved the whole Rebel army from outside Atlanta, where they took a good whuppin', and marched it up to the Tennessee River. Looks like they may be planning to come on up towards Nashville. A lot of good men fell in that Atlanta fight, and they have to fill out their ranks. That means me and you and a bunch of other county boys have got to go. They rode into town yesterday and have patrols out rounding up anybody who can carry a gun, load a cannon, or dig a hole."

William stared at him open-mouthed. "Mr. Ambers, I am all we got here. Pa's gone to fight for the Yankees, Ma's not strong, and Becky and Jim are just kids. I could fight, you know that, but Pa made me promise to stay here and look after things. We don't even know if Pa's still alive. You'd think we'd have heard something from him if he was able to get word to us. He's left us all alone here."

"I know, William, I know. Look at me. I've only got one arm, and I've got to go," Mr. Ambers said. "We've got no choice this time. Our only hope is that we go and survive and get back here before the planting starts in the spring. I've seen army life and it's hard, but the South just can't have much more fight left in her if they're coming for folks like you and me. I'm not sure they wouldn't take Jim if they could. We've got to fill out the levy here and that's all there is to it. Those men I'm riding with," he gestured out to the riders waiting patiently by the gate, "are hard men. They're Forrest's men," referring to General Nathan Bedford Forrest's notorious cavalry, "and you don't say no to men like that. Our best hope now is that we go with them and head down into Alabama. We could pull guard duty on a wagon train for the next five months and pray this war will be over by May."

Ma called out from the house as Becky and Jim brought a basket out to the porch.

"What's going on William," Ma called. "Is that your Pa come back?"

"No Ma," William called back, weariness and a touch of anger in his voice. "Pa ain't here, it's just me like always."

"I don't mind going, Mr. Ambers. It's going to be hard on Ma and the kids, but they'll survive. I've got to get off this farm and out from under all these chores. I've got to see the world and make my mark on it. I'm meant to be a soldier, and I can do anything my Pa can do. I can't believe he's left me to do all his work while he's off runnin' around without a care in the world."

"Becky," he turned to his sister, "you draw a pail of water for them and give it to Jim when he gets back." He then took a heavy breath and spoke quietly to Mr. Ambers. "I guess I have no choice, right? Ma is going to go crazy. But I know men like that mean to get what they came for." He glanced toward the waiting riders. "If we go quickly, will they leave the farm alone? We've got to leave enough food here for Ma and the kids to eat. Whether I like it or not they're still my responsibility."

Mr. Ambers took a biscuit and gave William an urgent look. William spoke quietly to his little brother. "Jim, take these biscuits to those men out there and watch your manners. Don't you say a dang word about Pa being a Yankee and you come straight back here." He pushed his little brother toward the riders.

"Yes, William, and you called it just right," Mr. Ambers said. "If we get your things and go with them quick, your family will be fine. The longer we dally, the more reason for them to come up here and take what they want. I'm sorry William, but we've got to go fast. Then we'll ride on to the next farm and be done here."

"What do I need, Mr. Ambers?" Excitement began to creep into William's voice. He was finally going to get away from this drudgery! "We don't have a horse or even a mule. I've been plowing with the milk cow. And this here gun is all we've got for rabbits and squirrels for the winter."

"Bring your best shoes and warmest clothes, William. Roll up some traveling food in your blanket and if you've got a decent canteen and hunting bag, bring them, too. Leave that rabbit gun for Jim, and for God's sake make it quick. By the time those riders finish their biscuits we've got to be ready to leave. They've got to find 50 men today, and they need to get moving. The faster they are away from here the better for your family."

William watched Jim walk up to the men with the basket, hand it to one of them, and turn to run back toward the house for the water. Jim was fascinated with soldiers, like William, and they had talked many nights in the loft where they slept about how they would be great soldiers some day.

And now, William was going to join their ranks and see the world beyond this dismal farm. His mother was going to howl.

CHAPTER 1
TROUBLE AT HOME

William's grandfather was one of those adventurous men who crossed the mountains and settled this land, carving the state of Tennessee out of the wilderness. He brought William's Pa out as a young boy, and John Sweeney didn't inherit the wander lust of his father. William resented the fact that his father had let this hard-scrabble farm become his life. William hated it.

Before he died, William's grandfather told wonderful stories of Daniel Boone and Davy Crockett, self-made men who faced the world head on. He thought of them as the role models he wished his father had become. Those men would never have let themselves become trapped in the mundane world of farming a patch of ground in this backwater of the world. William's imagination carried him to fancier places than the banks of Mulberry Creek that ran through their little farm and then on to the mighty Tennessee River just two days walk south.

William and his friends from the surrounding hills played together at the small school house they attended sporadically, as most farm kids with more work than time on their hands seemed to do. They saw each other at market days and county fairs, and attended church at the little building in town that served their community. Fayetteville, the small county seat with its mill and small stores, was the farthest William and any of his friends had ever been. All the local people called it "Fayettetown." Its dusty main thoroughfare heading toward Nashville was the gateway to many imaginary adventures for William.

Because his Pa had carved much of his farm out of rough country before William was old enough to work, William never seemed to have the same love of the farm that his father had. For William it was all work and very little excitement, and it caused tension between William and his Pa. Every day they would argue about the chores William would have to do.

When the sounds of secession came in the spring of 1861, William's Pa was astounded that something might disrupt this quiet, productive life he had built. How could men raise such a ruckus over things so distant? He owned no slaves, cared little for politics, and the debates stirring the nation to war seemed far removed from his little corner of the South.

William, however, reveled in the excitement and energy of the upcoming war. The mules became mighty chargers, and the rows of corn his advancing battalions. He cared little for the politics of the war, which he barely understood, he just wanted to get off this farm and fulfill his destiny of becoming a great man. No dirt farm lay in his future, that was for sure, and so what if his Pa seemed to agonize about the reality of this war coming. For William it was all exciting!

Big issues certainly drive the lives of little men. John was 35 when the guns roared at Fort Sumter in Charleston Harbor, an old man to be a soldier. William was just a boy of eleven, and the war gripping the nation provided him with endless hours of fantastic thoughts and flag waving glory. Even though the front lines were hundreds of miles away in Virginia and in northern Tennessee, William's mind took him there daily.

William and his father watched local men march off to join the newly formed Confederate army. They witnessed a brand new Tennessee regiment form and march out of Fayetteville one market day in 1861. William's father was against the war, which he thought was being fought for slavery and the rich men who owned them. The Sweeney's didn't own slaves and William had more than once heard his father speak out against the new country being formed. John felt it was not their fight.

The only slaves William knew belonged to his friend Louis Nix who lived down in the flatland part of the county beside Fayetteville. Louis didn't have to do all the work that William did on his farm, because he had three black slaves that did his work for him. Louis had a way of lording this over the other boys they ran with.

The government in Washington was too far from their lives for him to care much either way about it, and his Pa cared much more for the farm and the crops than the politics of the larger country. William worried when his father expressed his feelings about the war, because in these politically charged times being on the wrong side of this issue could get a boy of eleven beat up fast in town by the boys cheering for the Rebels, as the new Confederate country's sympathizers called themselves.

William helped his Pa bring in a good crop in 1861, and he knew they got good prices in town from the Army buyers. He heard his Pa grumble about the new Confederate and Tennessee State Notes they received as payment, but the local merchants seemed fine with the new paper, and the talk around the local gossip spots was that the war would be over this year.

By 1862, things seemed to take a turn for the worse in Tennessee. News came fast of the Confederate defeats at Fort Henry and Fort Donelson, and when Nashville fell to the Union, the war began to loom much closer. When William heard that the Rebel Army had retreated all the way into Mississippi, and that Union gunboats were prowling the Tennessee River west of Muscle Shoals,

Alabama, he began to think that the war would be over before he was old enough to get in it.

One day, William was plowing with the mule and daydreaming about leading his personal armies in great adventures when his father walked out to the road at the approach of a rider in the distance.

"William," his Pa said to him as he looked at the wandering rows his son had plowed, "what in the world have you been doing out here. Can't you get those rows any straighter? They're crookeder than a dog's hind leg!"

William threw down the lead in disgust. "Pa, it looks just fine! I'm twelve years old now and I know what I'm doin'. It'll plant just fine!"

"Don't you argue with me boy," his Pa said as the anger boiled up in him, "if you're going to do something, do it right. There's a rider coming and when he's gone, do it over. You're not big enough that I can't still take the strap to your backside if you talk back to me again!"

"Why can't we get a slave to do this plowing for us," William said, "how come we're not rich enough to get some help around here besides me?"

"You know I don't believe in slavery, son. It's not our place to own another man, and you've got to pull your own weight in this world and do it well," William's father was always amazed at the lengths his son would go to avoid a little work. It made him angry at what he perceived as his son's laziness.

As the rider came closer, William and his Pa glared at each other, but said no more. They both knew that it was dangerous to discuss these issues in front of others.

Daniel Sweeney reigned in. The other Mr. Sweeney was William's uncle, his Pa's brother. He wore a worried look on his face. William knew he had two sons with the Confederate army.

" Hello John, William," He said in nodded greeting. "There's been a big battle west of here at a place called Shiloh Church. My boys are out there and I mean to take a wagon over and make sure they're alright. Word is there's lots hurt and killed. John, I'd be obliged if you could go with me?"

"Sure Dan," William's Pa said. "I'm sure the boys are fine." The concern on his face belied the worry he also began to feel.

"Take me with you Pa," William cried, "I can be a help."

"No son, you stay here and tend the farm. This might be awful bad," his father said.

"You don't let me do anything fun!" William wailed, and he stomped his foot on the ground.

"I see you've got a spunky young man there, John," Daniel Sweeney said, a small smile playing across his face.

"I've got a spoiled little brat," John answered. "You listen to me boy," he said turning his angry gaze to William, "you do what I tell you. You're just a kid, and your place is here doing this work, and don't you give your Ma no trouble whilst I'm gone."

William sparked the mule and took off plowing. His Pa didn't know anything about what he could do. He'd show him someday, if he could ever figure a way off this blasted farm!

Word had spread quickly of the small community's loss. Several local sons and husbands lay dead on that field, and dozens more were horribly wounded. William's Pa joined his brother Daniel and four other older men of the county to take their farm wagons over to Shiloh to collect the wounded men from the county. They brought back the wounded from the hastily set-up field hospitals, and had to bury several of them on the return trip. John Sweeney vowed he would do all he could to keep his family out of this war. They never did find one of Daniel's sons.

William, however, thought it was the most exciting thing ever. He plied his Pa with a thousand questions upon his return, and could not understand his silence on the subject. He figured Pa didn't say anything about it just to spite him.

The few spare moments William had were spent playing Rebels around the farm, and William carved his little brother Jim an exceptionally detailed toy rifle. Pa rode William even harder with work on the farm to try to run the play out of him. Pa knew this was no time to be thinking of false glory. He knew war was only horrible.

One day their sister, Becky, was playing nurse to the two pretend-wounded boys, and was bandaging their mock bullet holes when their father walked onto the back porch where they were playing. In a fit of rage, Pa tore off their bandages, broke Jim's toy rifle, and for the first time in their young lives, swore. Their mother, Ida, rushed to them from the kitchen and softly quieted their father. The children learned never to mention the war again around their Pa.

After that, William hid his romantic visions of the war and his pretend battles away from his father. But he resolved to get in the big show somehow himself, no matter what his father thought.

CHAPTER 2
THE TROUBLE WITH WORK

Ida carefully spooned the grits onto the family's plates early one summer morning in 1863. The sun was not yet up, and John, William, and Jim would soon be on their way to the fields. A late night thunderstorm had turned the fields soupy and it was going to be a long day.

"I made a little bacon for you today, dear," Ida said to John, and glanced up to see the small smile play over her husband's face.

"Now ain't that the way to start the day!" John exclaimed, smiling back. He tussled Jimmy's hair and said "It'll do these boys good to get some meat on their bones. We'll be so dirty by the time we get back you won't recognize these two rascals!"

William rolled his eyes.

Becky, now 11, had been helping Ma in the kitchen and was making a frightful racket with the skillet and a spoon as her little hands struggled to clean off the cooked-on grease, so it took the family a minute to notice the dogs barking. As John and William began to push their chairs away from the table, and little Jim reached for his brother's bacon, they all heard a tremendous explosion outside and saw the front door fly back on its hinges from the force of a powerful kick.

There, standing in the doorway, were two dirty, unshaven, hard-eyed men in blue coats.

"What's fer breakfast!" yelled the one with the smoking carbine, the tallest and broadest of the pair. The other blue-coat aimed his pistol at Pa's chest as they walked into the room.

In a split second, all the children and Ma were cowering behind Pa, who eased himself up from the table with his hands fully visible. Pa took a deep breath, and let it out slowly even though adrenaline raced through his body. He knew these might be his most important words ever.

"Good morning, gentlemen, we've been expecting you. Ida, why don't you and the children go to the cellar and get some more bacon for our guests." He looked questioningly at the intruders.

"That'll be fine, friend," the big Yankee said to Pa. "We're real sorry to have startled you fine folks, but it's hard times for all and we never know what to expect when we come calling. Anybody else here?"

"Just us in this room, Sergeant," Pa said, noticing the three chevrons on the man's sleeve. He nodded slightly to Ma behind him as the big Yankee motioned for them to go. Ma, Becky, and Jim scurried to the cellar, but William stood his ground next to his father.

"Nice lookin' family you got there, Mister...."

"Sweeney," Pa said, "John Sweeney." Pa did everything he could to relax the taunt muscles in his neck and shoulders without moving, trying to calm the situation. William pointed to the stove and said, "Can I get you some plates, Mister?"

"Sure, boy. That'd be nice." The big Yankee sergeant turned his head and shouted outside, "looks peaceable enough in here. One man and his boy, and the wife and two kids in the cellar. Keep a sharp eye and we'll send out some grub."

"Sure, Sarge," a voice came from outside.

The smaller Union soldier kept his pistol on Pa and a wary eye on William, but seemed to visibly relax. The big Yankee sat down at William's place at the table and deftly shoveled a spoonful of grits into his wide mouth.

"Sit down, Mr. Sweeney. We're all farmers, just like you. We've had a couple years of living the hard life and our manners ain't what they used to be. Sit down, Mr. Sweeney, sit down. You're woman and kids are safe enough. We mean you no harm. We just want some vittles and feed our horses, and then we'll be on our way."

"There's not much here, mind you," said Pa, "but we'll spare you what we can. Jim, bring up that side of bacon we were saving for next month. Ma'll show you which one." They could hear the frantic whispers downstairs as Ma, Becky, and Jim rummaged through the darkness for bacon. William filled two new plates for the soldiers inside, and asked, "How many outside?"

"Just set the skillet outside, son, and they'll help themselves." Turning to Pa, he said "What we're really after, Mr. Sweeney, is you. You may have heard there's a war going on out there," he gestured expansively with a big meaty hand toward the door," and Uncle Abe feels you might just be the man to help him out. We're East Tennessee men, and by our coats you can see we're thrown in with the Federals."

"There's a big push into Georgia this year, and we need some strong men like yourself to come give us a hand. We're forming up some Tennessee regiments to pull some real light duties, like guarding against those thieving Forrest men, so it'll be nice and safe. We could use a man like you to come join us. We feel bad, of course, taking you away from hearth and home and all that, but we see you've got a strong lad there," he motioned toward William, "to help out at home until you get back. Just a few months and you'll be back in the lap of luxury."

John couldn't believe his ears. William froze in his tracks and their eyes met.

"The way we see it, Mr. Sweeney, is like this. You come with us nice and peaceable, and since you are from then on an O-ficial Union man, your family and property are now under Federal protection. But iffen you decide NOT to join our little adventure, well, we'll just have to say you're a rebel sympathizer and take action accordingly." He leaned forward on his elbows across the table toward John for emphasis. "Come with us, John, and your boy can look after things for you for awhile. Your farm and family will remain intact, and you'll be home soon enough."

He leaned back and shoveled another mouthful of food in. "Mr. Sweeney, these Rebs ain't got much fight left in them. You'll be home by Christmas with a pocketful of Yankees dollars."

John took a deep breath, held it, and exhaled slowly. William could see his brain churning, but he remained very calm. "How long do I have?"

"I'd say until my men finish that slab of bacon your boy is bringing up from the cellar." He said the last part very loud, and Jim, scurrying in, gave the bacon to William and ran back to the cellar.

"Pa, you can't go fight with the Yankees!" William said, his mouth once more running before his brain engaged. "And you can't leave me here alone to run all this by myself. It ain't fair!"

"You hush yer' mouth boy, 'for we shut it fer' ya' and plug yer' Pa to boot," the big Yankee sergeant said.

Pa looked wildly at William. "Please William, just for once do what you're told and keep your mouth shut. You've got to become a man now, son, and take care of things. It's up to you to do what's right and not take the easy way out of everything."

The big Yankee suddenly roared with laughter. "I see you've got a troublesome boy at home too. Well, he'll learn soon enough what it means to work hard around here, won't you boy!" He looked hard at William. "And you best keep yer' politics to yer' self with me around. The South's about done and you'll be on yer' own to do all this work!"

Pa leaned down to William. "Son, you've got to step up and do your best around here. We're all counting on you. Your Ma will need you more than ever."

"It just ain't fair, Pa!" William spat, "You get to run off and leave me with all the work while you get to go play soldier. I'll be a worn out old man never havin' done nuthin' by the time you get back. I'll never git off this farm!"

"Maybe so William," Pa soothed, trying to keep William's temper down in front of the strangers. "But I'll be back as soon as I can to take back over here."

"You just go on off and fight with them Yankees and don't mind comin' back!" William shouted through welling tears of frustration. "I'm getting out of here just as soon as I can and you can't stop me now."

Pa's hand slashed backwards across William's cheek and knocked him to the floor. He stood over his son. "You do like I say boy, and I will be back, and I'm counting on you to keep this farm together. You're going to learn someday not to talk back, and that being a man is not about what's over the next hill but what needs doing right in front of you. Do that and you'll become a man. Grow up son, there's no time left."

And with that, Pa was gone.

CHAPTER 3
BOY IN CHARGE

The next year without Pa was terrible. Ma became frightfully afraid anytime the dogs began to howl. Her health deteriorated, and the children had to work extra hard to help out. William grumbled every step of the way. He did just enough to keep food on the table. With little Jim and Becky's help he finally got the crops in the ground, kept the animals fed, and did as much as he could to keep the farm running. He knew he was going to spend the war cooped up in this cursed farm. The world was going to pass him by!

Times became much harder. It was not uncommon any more for army foraging parties of a couple of wagons and twenty or thirty men to come though the county collecting provisions. They sometimes paid with promissory notes, and sometimes even real Yankee dollars or Confederate notes, but several times bands of riders had come through and stolen what they wanted.

Ma was terrified of these visits and had almost stopped being of sound mind, and William had to learn to hide what they needed to keep the farm going. The family chicken coup was way back in the woods and William had to go there every day by a different route to keep a trail from showing. He had to build it very strong using floorboards from the barn to keep the predators out. Becky watched them most days and they left two dogs tied up there at night.

He staked the only remaining cow on the other side of the woodlot out back and he worried constantly about her safety. It was extra hard work taking care of her so far away. The pigs were just gone; sold or stolen over the last year. Powder for the rabbit gun was in pretty good supply, however, because the soldiers always traded a little powder and shot with him for the game he killed. Ma and Becky also knitted scarves for the soldiers to use as bandages and to keep the dust off their faces, and that gave them something to trade for currency. They could count on a visit or two per month from these foraging parties. It was awful for William to watch these soldiers ride away without him.

The family had not heard a word from John Sweeney since he left. No letters meant bad news, and it made William angry that his father had left him to fend for the family and hadn't found a way to get word back to them that he was safe. His mother was always distraught over this, but since Fayetteville was still in Rebel territory it was possible letters from a Yankee soldier couldn't get through.

The scariest things for them were the groups of rangers that roamed the back roads. They were raiders and ambushers that preyed on the organized foraging parties. These were hard men from the fringes of both armies, and many times were no better than thieves and murderers. Both sides had them, and they caused great consternation in the counties of the South touched by war.

William and Jim had tunneled out a place for their Ma and Becky to hide when these men came through, and they built a false wall for them that covered the place almost perfectly.

Their mule had been stolen on one of these frightful days when the rangers came. They were warned by the dogs barking quick enough for Ma and Becky to hide, and William manned the locked door with Jim watching the back.

The mule, William thought! He had gotten lazy that day and forgotten to hide the mule in the woods. He could have kicked himself for not secreting her away that night, because now she was gone for sure!

The riders had approached from behind the barn so William didn't see them coming. He had the cow and chickens hidden, but he had just brought the mule into the barn for the night because he was tired.

The riders fired two quick shots at the house, and then yelled that they were taking the mule and some forage from the barn.

"Take her!" said William, his blood boiling, "but come near the house, and I'll plug you!"

"Okay, son'" the rider yelled back. "We'll leave you a little coffee and some powder for the mule. You got any whiskey in that house?"

"No sir," William yelled back. "You'll find some jerky in a tin box in the barn I put there for times like this. You're welcome to it."

"You're a smart boy, son" the rider called back. "I hope my boy back home in Indiana is as smart as you! We hate to take your mule, son, but we need her. You'll just have to make do."

Most of the men William came in contact with this way weren't really bad men, though you could never tell. He'd heard stories about bushwhackers out in Missouri who burned out a farm for the sport of it. People said it was awful war out there, small bands of cavalry fighting back and forth in a wild no-man's land of shifting loyalties and bloody feuds.

Around here, these were mostly Tennessee and Alabama men from the South, and Indiana and Illinois men from the North, who had farms back home they cared about deeply. For the most part they tried to respect the land they fought over.

One day a troop of regular Confederate cavalry came through on a raid heading north. The Sweeney cabin was not on a regular road so they didn't have it as bad as some folks, but there was a track that cut through their valley following Mulberry Creek. William was sowing seed in the field one day right by the road when he saw three sets of riders approach, one set in the road, and one each on either side about a quarter mile out east and west.

As the pair of gray horsemen in the road approached William, they paused beside him.

"Seen any Yankees 'round these parts, young general?" One of the men asked William. William noticed he was a young man, not much older that himself. He wore a threadbare gray jacket, and stuffed in his belt were two large horse pistols. They were huge compared to his small frame. Over his shoulder, tied by leather strap, was a short Cavalry carbine. He wore a small gray cap jammed on his head. He looked like he was born in the saddle.

"Nope," William said truthfully. "Where ya'll headed?" he then asked.

"We're off to pull Abe Lincoln's beard" the young man said and laughed easily. He asked William how far to the next crossroads, then to Fayetteville, and if he knew of any Yankee activity lately. William told him quickly about the mule, and the young cavalryman said "Those scalawags! If we find yer mule, and she ain't 'et already, we'll bring her to you on the way back. Take care little brother," and with that, he rode away.

Five minutes later, a regiment of 300 Confederate horsemen rode by William. The dust cloud they kicked up was enormous! They rode four abreast, and the colonel up front by the battle flag tipped his hat to William as they rode by. Men rode by for what seemed like an hour. Halfway down the column two small horse-drawn cannon rolled by with men riding on the caissons and two men on the pulling horses. Their carriage wheels made an awful squeaking noise. William could see shadowy gray riders off to the sides of the column behind him and on the other side of the road protecting against ambush.

At the tail of the column came two sturdy farm carts pulled by mules. A one-legged man drove one and two Negro men the other. All three waved to William as they drove by.

As he watched the Confederate column disappear down the lane, William wished, for about the millionth time, that he could get off this back breaking farm and become a soldier. Three weeks later, Mr. Ambers rode up to his front gate in the early morning mist - and suddenly he was one.

CHAPTER 4
THE NEWEST REBELS

By the end of the day he was taken, William had walked many miles. Since he owned no horse or mule, he walked behind the riders. They had picked up eleven others from surrounding farms, mostly young boys like William and old or crippled men like Mr. Ambers. The group had divided itself up pretty quickly. Two veterans with horses had joined Mr. Ambers and rode with the soldiers. They each had butternut-colored coats from their previous time as Confederates, but each also bore other marks of the veteran. One had half his cheekbone and ear shot away and a terrible scar remained. The other had no left hand.

William's group consisted of farm boys. They were young, mostly 14, 15 and 16, but they were tough. Even though the short, wrenching departure was unsettling to them all, by evening the exuberance of youth and the promise of adventure was getting the better of them. William walked along with Louis Nix, the 15 year old boy he knew from town who owned the slaves. They had been acquaintances their whole lives, but had never really been close. Louis was several inches shorter than William, and had a round, somewhat pudgy face. He was one of the only boys in the group who had a softness to him, mostly from being a kid whose slaves did his work instead of himself.

Not that anyone had an easy life out here in the low hills of south Tennessee, just that Louis had led an easier life than William. Louis' mother doted on him, and William could imagine the scene when her baby was hauled off to war. Louis' brother was in Virginia with General Lee, and his father was in Mobile at Fort Morgan. You had to admit, no matter what you thought of the slave-owning Nix family, they had certainly offered up their blood for their new country's defense. Louis, however, was the bottom of their barrel.

Louis' brother had brought him back a Confederate cap when he was home last year, and he was wearing it now. He felt that the cap put him in charge of the other boys, and, as he and William walked at the front of the little column, Louis kept up a steady stream of conversation. "Okay boys," Louis said, "the first thing we have to learn you young'uns is how to march. My brother said they do it 'hay foot, straw foot' 'cause ya'll mostly don't know your left from your right. They tie hay to one foot and straw to the other, so you know which is which." He raised his right hand. "Everyone raise your hand like me." About half the boys raised their arms. Some glowered at him. The veterans looked at each other sideways and grinned.

Louis kept up this chatter all the way to Fayetteville. As they came down Main Street they saw on the steps and in the yard of the small courthouse about sixty other men and boys just like themselves, some standing in a line and others milling around talking. One of the soldiers with Mr. Ambers said, "Ambers, this is your squad. Take 'em up to that line there and sign in."

Mr. Ambers led the group to an officer sitting on the courthouse steps who made them stand and raise their hands and swear allegiance to the Confederate States of America. He wrote their names on a roll of paper, had them make their mark or sign their names, and welcomed them to the glorious Army of Tennessee.

The officer called all the men and boys together and made a short speech about the great tradition of the fighting force they were joining. While he spoke, a huge kettle of stew was simmering behind them. Several of the ladies of Fayetteville had started this supper for the troops, and were busily getting ready to serve them when the officer finished talking.

William was famished and thought it smelled wonderful! He looked sideways at Louis and motioned with his eyes toward the stew. They were planning to be first in line!

At the exact moment William looked toward the pot of steaming stew he saw a gray-clad rider galloping pell-mell down the street toward them. He heard him call, "Alarm! Alarm! Yankee cavalry!" over and over as he reigned in his lathered horse at the feet of the officer. William caught the words on the air as every ear strained to hear. "Yankee cavalry, sir! Heading this way! At least…a troop… one hour away… had to leave my recruits!"

The officer turned to the newly sworn in soldiers. "Men, we have one wagon and just a few horses, so we are going to have to quick march out of here. You are soldiers now, and I expect no stragglers. Grab your gear, as we march in five minutes with no time to spare. Deserters, of course, will be shot." And with that, he turned on his heel and started the movement of his little company.

William and Louis ran and grabbed their meager possessions and looked longingly at the kettle of stew they knew they would not taste. The recruiting soldiers were busy pushing the men into formation and organizing the march. Within five minutes, true to the officer's word, they were on the move heading to Alabama and the waiting Army of Tennessee.

They slept in a small patch of woods well after dark six hours down the road.

"No fires, boys," the officer commanded. "Each squad will maintain a sentry at all times in case of alert. Keep it quiet tonight, boys. We'll be in our picket lines by tomorrow night."

William and Louis were awakened a few hours later for their watch. They were well off the road, but that night they could see shadows of mounted men on the road searching for them. They turned to see Mr. Ambers motioning them to be very quiet, and the horsemen passed without incident. William was too scared to sleep any more that night. He had hunted game his whole life, but never been hunted himself!

William stood in a soft pine thicket. Needles from the trees gave him cover from their pursuers and something to chew on while his mind wandered. He would become a great soldier and ride back into Fayetteville a hero now that he was going to the army. He would show his Pa he was a man that could make his own decisions.

Just before sunrise the veteran soldiers moved quietly among the raw recruits, shaking everyone awake. William fell in behind Mr. Ambers. Louis had a harder time getting his things together, but puffing, caught up with him and walked beside him. Louis looked like he had been crying, and William was sure he had heard more than a few whimpers from him last night in the darkness.

Their little column moved west, away from the main road. The veterans were old hands at moving like this and the new recruits were too scared, cold, and hungry to make much noise, so the column moved silently westward until they finally turned south on a small farm track.

At midday they stopped at a crystal clear brook and watered the horses and men and rested for a few minutes. The weather was turning colder and gray clouds hung heavy in the sky.

"This has been the darndest walk I've ever been on," said Louis quietly, his breath showing in the cool air.

"I know it's the longest time I've ever heard you quiet," William whispered.

"William, you just don't know a brilliant conversationalist when you hear one," Louis said, getting his bluster back up and receiving a sharp "hush" from Mr. Ambers.

William helped Mr. Ambers unsaddle and rub his horse down. Mr. Ambers was pretty good with only one arm, but having help was always nice for him. The pleasure of helping Mr. Ambers reminded William of the end of the day with his Pa back in better times. A small patch of sunlight came through the cloud cover and warmed him.

"We could be in for a few rough miles here, William," Mr. Ambers said. "I've always liked your family and your Pa is a good man. I know he had to join the Yanks when they came through, and I know you and he didn't exactly see eye to eye on lots of things. I'd keep that information close to your vest. No need for trouble from that quarter if you can avoid it. He's not the only man that got caught up in that raid, but silence is your best option. You stick close to me and if there's trouble we can't avoid you hop up here in the saddle with me. I've been in some mighty tight scrapes in this war, and I know when to stand and when to run. Here son, I want you to carry a dozen of these cartridges for my horse pistol. I can shoot pretty well with my left hand but I'll be darned if I can reload. If we get in a fight I'll toss the pistol down to you and you reload it."

He showed William how to reload the big Navy Colt he carried in his belt, and William looked at the dozen cartridges in his hand. Louis peered over his shoulder and William gave him an irritated glance.

"Keep 'em dry boy," Mr. Ambers said, and he handed William a small oilskin cloth to wrap them in. "Above all else keep that powder dry." William thought about his uneven rows of corn and the lost mule, and felt a little nervous for his first big responsibility in the army. He would do well with this, he decided, and show his Yankee dad that he could fight with the best of them.

"Louis, you stay close too," Mr. Ambers said. "I promised your Ma I'd get you home safe." Louis looked at him pleadingly, and then seemed to buck his spirits up and nodded his head.

About an hour after they moved past the little stream they heard firing off to the east. Just a shot or two at first, then it seemed to take off like a big thunderstorm of gunfire. A few minutes later it slowly died down. William found himself walking with Mr. Amber's horse between him and the firing. It was an unconscious reaction and the fear it signaled embarrassed William.

The officer hurried the men into a patch of woods and had them hunker down. Most of the men were unarmed, and the officer's job was to get them to the army, not into a fight.

The officer sent two scouts out, one toward the gunfire and the other down the track to the river. Twenty minutes later they both returned, moving so silently that they were back in the thicket before William even heard them. As they began to move south again, word passed down the ranks that Confederate cavalry had skirmished with the Yankees hunting them along the main road. They were starting to come under the protection of the Rebel Army.

Around dusk they met another column of recruits, just like themselves, on the road, and after dark they finally reached a small cavalry camp with another couple hundred unarmed men and a troop of cavalry guarding it. They got their first meal in two days.

William's thoughts again strayed to his family back on the farm. How were they going to survive? He had been all they had, and now they had to fend for themselves. Where was his Pa? Was he even still alive? Was he out there with that Federal cavalry, looking for him even now. William thought about the last day they had been together, and the harsh words they had exchanged. He thought about having to hide the fact that his Pa fought for the Yankees. What would these men do to him if they found out? Would they think him a spy?

While William worried, he began to notice that the veteran cavalry troopers were taking the fresh mounts of the men who had ridden in, including Mr. Ambers. They also took all the men's shoes and boots and blankets and gave them their old worn out ones. William's warm homemade quilt, made by his Ma years ago, was traded to a snaggle-toothed private for a threadbare army-issue scrap of cloth full of holes. His shoes also were taken, replaced by a worn-out pair of leather brogans with holes completely through the soles. They even took his socks!

This didn't happen forcefully, or officially; it just happened. Old campaigners like Mr. Ambers expected it and were prepared. When this sanctioned robbery was completed, William went to Mr. Ambers to complain.

"Sorry boys, that's just the way it is. We'll be going back to the rear tomorrow to get formed with a new regiment. These boys in the cavalry never get to the rear. This will happen again once we get to our new unit, and if we live long enough, we'll do it to new recruits someday ourselves. It's been like this since the Romans, and it'll always be like this. Rebel soldiers like these here men either take their kit from the countryside or from the enemy, and right now we're still part of the countryside."

That night William shivered as the winds of late autumn blew down on their camp. He slept with an eye open to make sure nothing else from his meager possessions disappeared in the night. This was not turning out to be the glory and pomp William had pictured in his day dreams. Where were the fine ranks of drilled men with fancy uniforms he thought he'd see? Where were the officers with their gold cuffs and braid? This was just like being at the farm, only terrifying.

The next day brought William into Alabama, and by nightfall the little column had reached the banks of the Tennessee River at

Muscle Shoals, a huge expanse of exposed river rock covered with mussel shells and lichen. This was one of the few spots where the rebels could cross the mighty river without the threat of Yankee gunboats. Bainbridge Crossing was protected on either side by this massive bank of shoals. Gunboats had been built on the eastern side of this part of the river and operated out of the Yankee stronghold at Chattanooga. On the western side of the shoals gunboats ran the river to Florence, just a few miles to the west. But right here, under the cannon of John Bell Hood's Army of Tennessee, crossings were as sheltered as they could be.

By the time William arrived at the crossing, their ranks had swollen to five or six hundred men and boys. Across the river from them lay a great camp of Confederates, many thousand strong. The campfires lit up the riverbank amid the swells and hollows like a large city. The sight awed William. Here at last was what he pictured an army to look like, and he would surely see here everything he had imagined.

William watched the ferry pull a steady line of men across the river. By the light of a frosty moon early in the morning, William and his small party crossed to the other side and dropped as soon as they found a dry spot, exhausted, hungry, and cold.

When the sun rose, a gravelly-voiced sergeant rousted the new recruits from their exhausted slumber.

William and Louis followed Mr. Ambers to form a line with the hundreds of other milling men.

"Listen up here and we'll assign you to your units. Your regiments will then come find you, so you sit tight once you know your unit. Don't ask no questions, do as you're told, and you'll get along famously!"

"Boys, you stay mighty close to me," Mr. Ambers said to his charges. I'll do my best to keep us all together." That was just fine with William, who stuck with Mr. Ambers like his shadow. There was something comforting about this quiet, crippled man that made William feel a little safer, even though Mr. Ambers had been responsible for putting him in this predicament.

"2nd Tennessee Cavalry" shouted the man at Mr. Ambers, Louis, William, and a few other boys from Fayetteville. Mr. Ambers dropped a small coin on the table in front of the sergeant and quietly said, "Give me these other lads from back home, Sarge. I promised their mothers I'd look after them."

The bored sergeant looked at Mr. Ambers' missing arm and said, "Take who you want and wait over there. Hope you keep the other arm with your bodyguard here." He winked at Mr. Ambers while pocketing the money. "Next!"

Mr. Ambers, like a good shepherd, kept his eleven Fayetteville boys together. He called them all to sit around him. "Boys, it's like this. Before long a sergeant will come along to get us. I felt it was important to keep us all together, but we must split up within the Regiment. I've seen one or two cannon blasts wipe out a whole company of men in less than a minute. So I want you to pair up, twos or threes, and stick together, no matter what. They'll assign us to companies that way. That way some of us for sure will make it back alive."

"Now, I can write a little, and Mr. Sims down at the post office back home can certainly read, so every week each one of you boys come see me wherever I am and let me know how you're doing. I'll write a letter to Mr. Sims each week and we'll do our best to keep your families knowin' how you are."

He turned to William and Louis. "You boys do your best to stick with me. We'll take a chance that with only one arm they'll put me on the company wagon and you with me. But it could go against us and I may have to carry the colors. I can do that with one hand, but they sure get shot down a lot. Like I say, we'll just have to take our chances."

And that's just how it worked out.

CHAPTER 5
THE REGIMENT

The Sergeant from the 2nd Tennessee came and picked up Mr. Ambers and his boys. William's heart sank as he walked through the camp of the army and saw how absolutely squalid everything was. No one had anything decent. Their clothes were all rags, their tents were mere scraps of cloth, but he did notice their rifles and bayonets gleamed with care. At their regimental camp they were separated, but Mr. Ambers, William, and Louis stayed together.

They went to Company A, 2nd Tennessee Cavalry and were introduced to their new commander, Captain John Richardson. He sat on the stump of a tree recently cleared and balanced some papers on his knee. He looked up with a kind face.

Captain Richardson was a handsome man with a large bushy mustache. His finely tailored uniform coat had seen better days, but his martial appearance spoke volumes. By this time in the war, captains were usually highly skilled soldiers and leaders. There were not any dandies left in this army.

"Welcome to A Company, men," Captain Richardson introduced himself. "We're glad to have you with us. We're sixty men now with you three. We started the Atlanta campaign with over 100. Those that are left are tough as nails. We're cavalry, but we don't have any horses left, so we kept the name and we fight as infantry, on foot. We've got plenty of rifles for you in the supply wagon, and there's bits and pieces of other equipment and uniforms in there. Help yourselves to what you can find."

"Mr. Ambers," the Captain said to the one armed man, "Are you a veteran?"

"Shiloh and Murfreesboro with the 44th Tennessee, Sir. I was a color sergeant, and lost my arm on the Wilkinson Road with Bushrod Johnson and Pat Cleburne."

"I remember that fight well. I was on the left with General Wharton's cavalry. You'll be glad to know that we are still with General Cleburne. Since we're not really cavalry anymore, he uses us mostly for scouts and skirmishers. We lost our supply sergeant to fever on the march from Atlanta, so we need a new man there. You're now Sergeant Ambers, so don't let me down. You have two mules with the wagon. Use these two farm boys," he gestured to William and Louis, "to help you with the animals. When we go into a fight, they'll be my runners, so make sure they learn all the sergeants and lieutenants in the company. I'll take them with me to Regimental Headquarters so they can meet the other runners there."

A sharp voice cracked like thunder behind Williams' ear.

"Stand up straight when you address the captain, you men!" The voice carried a small sapling stick that popped Louis on the back of the shoulders. Stand up straight there, Private."

"Sorry sir, just trying to round us up some grub. Not much to be found around here. These the new recruits, sir?" the voice asked the Captain. William could feel eyes drilling in to him from behind. "A one-armed cripple and two school boys? We're scraping the bottom of the barrel now aren't we sir?

"Take care of these men, First Sergeant, and see they're added to the rolls. I have made Sergeant Ambers here our supply sergeant and assigned him and these two boys to the wagon." Captain Richardson then returned to the paperwork on his knee.

First Sergeant Dillard was the meanest looking man William had ever seen. The first thing you noticed about Dillard were his eyes. One looked directly at you and was coal black and piercing. The other, slightly askance, bore a scar straight down the middle so that his eyelid never quite closed in the center. The scar ran from his hairline to the corner of his mouth and was bright red. William had the feeling that eye could peer directly into his soul.

His hair was long and scraggly and hung wildly from under his cap. His neck and shoulders were incredibly broad, but his hands were the things you noticed most. They were massive and powerful and stuck out of his uniform coat like two huge ham hocks. Dillard had a menacing air to him. He always stood just a little too close, and he seemed to produce a thin spray of spittle when he spoke.

Dillard walked Ambers and the boys to the wagon, snarling at them.

"I see you've met our nice Captain, boys. Well don't you think for one minute you are anything but mine now." He leaned close to mister - now Sergeant - Ambers. "You step out of line and I'll see you lose that other arm. You take good care of my mules on that wagon, and you better get good at foraging food for us, or there'll be hell to pay. Our last wagon master was a worthless sod and was always running off and leaving us hungry. He thought he was beyond my control back there safe behind the firing line."

Dillard turned his gaze to the boys and glowered at them. "And you two: Nix, you look soft, like you've been pampered your whole life; and Sweeney, if I've sized you up correctly, you're a problem waiting to happen. I don't see any discipline in either of you. When you're running for the Captain you better flat run and you better get things right. Our lives will depend on it. If you don't, I'll have you in the front rank stopping bullets."

They reached the wagon, if you could call it that. William had never seen a more tumbledown contraption or two more pitiful looking mules in his whole life. The tack was crumbling leather but William noticed the buckles were shiny and looked freshly polished. Just then, a bundle of rags under the wagon moved and from it emerged a small black face, about the same age as William. The face then broke into a wide grin, crooked teeth glistening.

"This here's Henry," Dillard snarled, gesturing his sapling at the boy emerging from under the blankets and stretching himself up to his full height. He was about Williams' height and a little taller than Louis. William noticed his feet were bare.

Henry nodded his head at the boys and at the two sergeants. "Pleased to makes your acquaintance, gentlemens," he said good-naturedly. Henry rocked a little from side to side as he spoke. Dillard swatted him on the side of the head with the sapling, but Henry didn't seem to notice.

"Henry came with the wagon when it was 'liberated' from a plantation in Georgia." Dillard said. "He's been with us for two years, and he keeps the mules fed. Seeing as how they're about half starved, ain't been doing too good a job have you Henry?"

Henry took obvious discomfort at this.

"Cain't find no forage, First Sergeant. I's been tryin' but just cain't find nuthin' fer' dese 'ol mules to eat." Henry looked at the ground. Then he brightened, pointing to the buckles. "How 'bout them buckles, First Sergeant? I worked 'em good this mornin'"

"They look fine Henry." Dillard said distractedly. "You help out these new boys here and get these mules fed, or I'll tan your hide again."

William had very little experience with colored folks. Louis was the only slave owner he had ever met, and he wasn't sure what to think of Henry. Louis, on the other hand seemed to visually sigh with relief when he saw there was a slave here to do his chores.

Their first night in the 2nd Tennessee bivouac was pleasant, if somewhat cold. Several of the men in the company came by to introduce themselves and see where these new men were from. Everyone was always looking for any news from home, and the soldiers that came by were happy to hear talk of farms and towns and a normal life they hadn't seen in a long time. The boys bedded down by the wagon after taking care of the mules, with Henry rubbing one down and William the other, while Louis kept up a constant stream of prattle and not doing much work. Ambers was right about the equipment they found in the wagon, however. They each found a little sturdier blanket and a haversack and canteen in the supply wagon.

William had to clean the blood off the cartridge box he found, and the best uniform coat he could find also had a hole the size of his finger in one sleeve below the elbow and a huge dark stain there. But it was warm and made him look a little more like a soldier than a misplaced farm boy.

Both William and Louis found rifles for themselves in the wagon, great big long guns with a place for a bayonet on the end. Since neither boy was very big they had been hoping for short cavalry carbines, but these big Enfields would have to do.

Because they were the new men, Sergeant Ambers and the boys started the next morning doing First Sergeant Dillard's dirty work. The boys had to comb the area for anything that would burn for the Captain and First Sergeant's fire and get a good blaze going. The temperature in the evenings was getting colder, and it took a yell from Dillard to get the boys away from the fire and back to rubbing down the mules.

Sergeant Ambers had a little fire going by the wagon when they got back.

"Get used to that boys," Ambers said. "This ain't no different than being on the farm. Keep the officer's fire going, rub down these mules, and bring some wood here for our fire. In a little while we'll hitch up the wagon and head over to the commissary and see if we can't round up some cornmeal and fat for the company."

Sergeant Ambers had been talking to some of the other men in the company to find out how things worked here. He had enough experience to know the basics, but he'd been out of the war for almost two years and this army was a lot different.

William and Henry hitched the mules to the wagon while Louis and Sergeant Ambers rearranged the equipment and stores in back. They had a mostly empty barrel of cornmeal, three big tin boxes of rifle cartridges, a dozen or so rifles, a wooden box of cups and pots, and some bits and pieces of old uniforms and cartridge boxes. This took up about half the wagon. The rest was usually filled with the officer's tents and the canvas shelters the men used, but was empty now.

Company A was camped on the side of a gently rolling hill. The captain's tent was in the center and the soldiers' tents radiated out from it like spokes in a wheel. The wagon was on the downhill side next to a small dirt track.

All around this little camp were hundreds just like it, as far as William could see. It was a lot more haphazard in appearance than he expected. There were still some trees standing, but all the fence rails had been burned in the campfires, and stumps of trees were visible everywhere. Morning mists hung low in the camps and William could see men shivering around feeble campfires.

First Sergeant Dillard strode up to Sergeant Ambers with a friendly looking man in tow. "This here's Corporal Heck," Dillard said. "He'll show you how to get over to Tuscumbia to see about some food for the company." He scribbled something on a small slip of paper with the barest scrap of a pencil and handed it to Ambers.

"We've been here a week and ain't hardly seen nothin' to eat." He moved close to Ambers' face menacingly. "I don't care how you find it, but you bring us some food back, you hear?"

With that, Dillard stalked off back to camp.

CHAPTER 6
OFF THE CLIFF

"Howdy boys," Corporal Heck said and stuck out his hand to each of them. "Don't mind Sergeant Dillard too much, now. He's a tough one all right, but he's fair if you do what you're told. He's been mean as a snake since his brother got killed at Kennesaw Mountain. We ain't had a lot of new men since then, so he's a mite strong getting' used to."

Heck climbed up on the wagon with Sergeant Ambers while William, Louis and Henry followed the wagon on foot. As they headed west toward Tuscumbia, Heck regaled them with stories from the last few months and filled in the pieces of what was coming.

"Back in September, we finally lost Atlanta to Sherman," Heck said. "We fought for that place for months, first under General Joe Johnston, and then General Hood. Fight and fall back, fight and fall back. When the city fell, old Hood took us all the way around behind the Yankees and we tried to cut their supply line, but we just couldn't bust through. So we backtracked down into Alabama to get our breath back. We've had some hard years, and we're worn out, but we reckon we got one more good fight left in us."

"We've been living off north Alabama crops for the last month, and our cavalry's out roundin' up boys like yourselves to help us. The rumor is that we're goin' up into Tennessee and take back Nashville. If we do that, boys, old Sherman will have to leave Atlanta and come try us again. We'll lick him for sure this time!"

William only half-listened to Corporal Heck's chatter. He watched, awe-struck, as the army camp rolled by. It was a bright, cold November morning, and as the sun arced high in the sky it glinted off thousands of stacked rifles.

There were tents everywhere, with thousands of men milling around them. William expected the camp to look different, with straight rows and orderly men. The camp looked like a giant hand had scattered men, campfires, wagons, tents, and mules all over the countryside.

"Look at all this mud," Louis said as they stared out over the bivouacs. "It tears me up to see all these good fields so rutted and fouled up by all these men. But it sure is a sight, ain't it William?"

William nodded his assent. From Bainbridge to Tuscumbia was about 5 miles. Several times the boys had to push the wagon out of huge mud holes. William was still wearing the worn out shoes he got at the cavalry camp, and his legs were soaked and freezing. He and Louis wrapped themselves in blankets and tried to stay warm.

Louis struck up a conversation with Henry.

"What'd you do back on the plantation there, Henry?" Louis asked in a casual sort of way.

"Wasn't rightly a plantation, mind you suh," Henry said. "Kind of a small place with maybe twenty of us folks workin' it. My Ma and Pa wasn't too happy with me takin' off with this here wagon, but the boss say go and I go'd. These folks treat me pretty decent, though the food's awful bad. There's plenty of us black folk workin' as teamsters an' such in this army, and some of the big officers has a servant they brung with 'em from home. You got slaves back home, suh?" Henry directed his question to Louis.

"We have three back home. One at the house cookin' with Ma and two helpin' me and my father with the farm. They've been with us as long as I've been alive. I'm sure it's home as much to them as it is to me." William thought Louis sounded a little smug.

William wondered at Louis' logic in this, and he glanced at Henry to see his reaction, but Henry just smiled and kept his thoughts to himself. William could hardly stand being on the farm and he wondered how it would be to be forced to stay there, with no hope of ever leaving. At least now that he was a grown man he could decide that on his own. Could Louis' slaves ever really decide their future?

Tuscumbia proved to be a pleasant town. It was filled with muddy soldiers, and had obviously seen better days than what three years of war had done to it, but William thought it was just marvelous. They watered the mules in a big spring just off downtown, and he, Louis and Henry waited for Sergeant Ambers and Corporal Heck to find the commissary.

They watched other empty wagons roll into town for the next hour while they waited. The streets were filled with ravenous looking men, wandering aimlessly searching for food. When Ambers and Heck finally came back, they both wore an air of despondency.

"There ain't nothing here boys," Sergeant Ambers said. "We've looked high and low, and can't find anything."

Corporal Heck chimed in, "Let's try down at the waterfront. Maybe there's something coming across on one of the ferries, and if we get to it first maybe we can get something for the company. We haven't had a decent ration in two weeks and we're starving!"

They piled in the wagon and headed north to the river. Tuscumbia's waterfront was busy as they approached. To their excitement, there was a ferry pulling in loaded with barrels coming over from Florence, but they weren't the only ones to see it. There was already a large crowd of soldiers taking away everything that was unloaded. Officers and sergeants shouted and teamsters hit starving men with barrel staves to keep some order to the chaos, mostly in vain.

A flat-bottomed raft pulled its way to shore loaded with about twenty barrels and boxes. As it pulled to shore a rush of men piled on board to grab what they could and threatened to swamp the boat. From the back of the crowd William stood on the wagon with the others to watch the spectacle. As the barrels at the front of the boat were man-handled off, the boat rocked and one of the barrels toppled off the side into water. The current was moving fast and took it quickly away, even as men plunged in the frigid water to try to catch it.

"Get that barrel, William!" Sergeant Ambers yelled. William jumped off the wagon and sprinted down stream, heading west as fast as he could run. "Get it to the bank William, and we'll find you!" Ambers yelled at his racing back.

The current was taking the barrel away quickly, so William had to think fast. To his left was a big hill with a towering rock bluff. The current slowed there, it seemed, so he sped up the hill as fast as he could go, trying to get ahead of it. He turned quickly to see Louis running behind. He was ten yards ahead of the barrel, now twenty, and he could see that the other men in the water had given up. By the time he reached the top of the bluff, he was well ahead of the floating keg, but he realized he was also sixty feet high on the bluff looking down!

William was an excellent swimmer from his days on Mulberry Creek, but this cliff was so high it made him gasp. He stepped to the edge, and with hundreds of eyes on him, he jumped off the bluff and into the water below.

When William hit the water, the shock of the fall and ice-cold river took his breath away. When he surfaced sputtering a moment later, he saw the barrel thirty yards behind and off to his right. He struck out ahead of it and caught it just as it came even with him. His fingers were already numb, but he held on to that barrel for dear life, and began to kick toward the river bank.

William heard Louis on the bluff above, and saw him motioning him downriver to a small cove about a hundred yards away. As Louis ran along the bluff, William kicked with all his might to get to the bank and out of this freezing water. His heart raced as he inched closer.

William was almost frozen by the time he felt Louis' hands pull him onto the bank with the precious barrel. He crawled on to dry ground with Louis at his side. They looked at each other and laughed as hard as they could.

"William, that was the most amazing thing I ever laid eyes on," Louis said as he struggled to his feet. "Come on, you've got to keep moving or you'll freeze to death.

He and Louis began rolling the barrel up the bank. They were in a thick tangle of trees and undergrowth, and it was difficult going, but eventually they came out on a small trail to find Corporal Heck grinning from ear to ear.

"Dang, boy!" Heck said, as he took over moving the barrel, "If that don't beat all!" You're going to be regular hero when we get back. A regular Hee-Row!"

A few minutes later they met Sergeant Ambers and Henry on the road. His big pistol was cocked beside him. "Get that barrel in here fast boys, and let's get back before somebody stops us!" Ambers said. He shot William an approving look and just shook his head from side to side. "If that don't beat all!" Corporal Heck kept saying, over and over.

They covered the barrel to hide it as best they could, but they couldn't hide poor soaked William. They had tried to dry him with a blanket they had in the wagon, but he was still shivering from head to toe. As they rumbled back past the waterfront, men began to point and cheer William's courage, and no one tried to take that barrel.

An officer rode up to them on a magnificent horse, and several more riders trotted behind. William noticed the officer's left arm was an empty sleeve, and that his right leg was just a stump. Because of that, he was strapped in his saddle.

"Good work, son," the officer boomed. "You give me hope for this Army, boy. With guts like that we'll lick those Yanks all the way to Ohio. He turned toward the men around him. "Let's hear it boys." The men let out the famous Rebel yell for William.

It was a sound he would hear again.

CHAPTER 7
BIG PLANS

General Hood lay on the cot his orderly had placed in his quarters. Hood had lost the use of his arm at Gettysburg with General Lee, and a few months later, he had lost his right leg above the knee at Chickamauga. He had recovered enough to lead an Army in the field, but the disappointment of the Atlanta campaign and his previous injuries had given him a weak constitution. He suffered so greatly from rheumatism that on some cold days he could barely rise.

Today had tried his spirits again. Watching the near riot at the waterfront and the desperate measures his men had to go to just to eat was disheartening.

Hood had moved from the ravaged countryside of Georgia to North Alabama, partly to rest and re-supply his army, but the promised supplies at Tuscumbia had proven illusory. Like everywhere in the Deep South, three years of war had stripped the countryside bare.

There came a rap at the door and the adjutant announced: "General Hood, your Corps Commanders are here, sir."

Come in, gentlemen," their commander said.

There was no love lost between Hood and his three primary subordinates. Each of these men commanded a third of his army. They were all professionals with plenty of battlefield experience, but John Bell Hood had never been an easy man to work for, and their experience around Atlanta had only made things worse.

General Alexander Stewart, General Ben Cheatham, and General Stephen Lee, had been corps or division commanders all through the Atlanta campaign, and it grieved then to see what the once proud Army of Tennessee had become. John Bell Hood was given command of the army halfway through the Atlanta campaign because the men in Richmond thought he would be more aggressive than General Joe Johnston, who seemed to be constantly retreating. Unfortunately Hood's aggressiveness only led to more casualties, and Atlanta fell anyway. For his part, Hood felt that part of the problem was that General Johnston had allowed the army to become used to doing their fighting from behind barricades and entrenchments. Hood felt that, because the Federal armies were so superior in equipment and numbers, the only way to have a chance of a Confederate victory was through sheer audacity and courage.

That's why he had moved his army to North Alabama.

"Gentlemen," Hood began, "we don't have the supplies to remain stationary very long. We've got to get this army moving north into Tennessee where we can live off the land and captured stores of the Federals."

"General Sherman has taken a large part of his army and is marching east from Atlanta to the sea. His army can't be stopped in the field with what we have, but we can, perhaps, pull him back north if we can capture Nashville. If our army can move north before General George Thomas can consolidate his scattered forces, we can defeat his smaller units in detail and, God willing, capture Nashville."

"We have reports of Federal forces being moved into the area around Pulaski. If this is true, however many they are, we must find them and defeat them. Then the way will be open to Nashville. Our ranks will swell as droves of men see our success and rally to us, and Middle Tennessee will be at our mercy! When we hold Nashville it will be like a dagger in the heart of Sherman, and he'll have to come back and fight us there. We can choose our ground carefully and he will batter his army on ours until it is destroyed."

Cheatham, Lee and Stewart listened to the plan unfold before them and were shocked at its optimism. It was breathtaking, that was for sure. They weren't sure if it would work, but it was certainly better than sitting on the Tennessee River watching their commands slowly starve and drift away.

"General Hood," Cheatham said, breaking the silence. "We've brought in about 3,000 recruits from our efforts here so far. Today is November 6th. From what we've heard, General Forrest's Cavalry won't be able to join us until at least the 14th, or there abouts. For your plan to work, we have got to move quickly. When do we march?"

Hood was pleased with these remarks. It seemed his generals were going to embrace his plan.

"Forrest's Cavalry will be on the north bank of the river when they arrive, and General Lee's corps already holds the area around Florence on that side. I plan on moving my headquarters across the river on the 13th and, General Cheatham, I want your corps to be ready to move with me. The supply train will follow as soon as possible and General Stewart's men will cross last. If we move north fast enough, we may be able to catch the Yankees at Pulaski off balance. Their defeat is the lynchpin of our entire plan. Get your divisions ready."

"General Cheatham," Hood continued, "once we are ready, you will take the Waynesboro Road and then strike northeast to Mount Pleasant. General Lee, you will have the center column and march north through Henryville and then move towards Mount Pleasant as well. General Stewart, you will march north on the Lawrenceburg Road and converge with the rest of our forces in the Mount Pleasant area. From there, it will be an easy day's march on the pike to Columbia. General Stewart, since you will be closest to the enemy, most of Forrest's cavalry will go with you and screen your advance. Speed is the key, gentlemen. If we can seize Columbia ahead of the Federals and trap them south of the Duck River, the battle of Nashville will be almost won. Prepare your commands to move, and God be with us!"

CHAPTER 8
AN IMPORTANT JOB!

William's return with the barrel of what turned out to be surprisingly good corn meal was exciting. Corporal Heck leapt off the wagon when they arrived and began to tell the story to the gathered soldiers. First Sergeant Dillard even slapped him on the back and said "Good job!"

Within minutes cooking fires around the camp sprang to life and Sergeant Ambers parceled out the ration to men looking for a hearty meal. William, however, was practically frozen. His wool clothes had remained cold and damp from his river plunge, and had not dried by the time they got back. To dry off, he and Louis huddled by Captain Richardson's fire, as it was the largest in camp.

"Congratulations, boys," the Captain said. "I hear you two are responsible for our rations this evening."

"Yes sir," Louis chimed in. "You should've seen William jump off that cliff sir! It was the darndest thing I ever saw!"

"That's what I'm looking for from you boys." The Captain motioned for them to join him. "You're going to be my runners in the upcoming battles, and it's going to take a lot of courage for you two to do your jobs. When we go into the firing line you stick close to me. It's loud, boys, and pretty quickly no one can hear commands by shouting. A regimental runner from the colonel will come to me with orders. Then I'll send you out to relay my orders to Lieutenant Jones, Lieutenant Dunn, and First Sergeant Dillard. They will then move the men into the positions I want.

I also may send you back to the Colonel if I have information for him. It sounds easy enough, but in battle it is deadly serious and frightening. You two have to stay focused on your jobs and not the hell going on around you."

"Are you boys dry enough to come meet the rest of the Company?" William and Louis nodded excitedly. They knew enough already that when the Captain suggested something, they were going to do it, and they had already taken quite a liking to this officer.

As Captain Richardson approached each campfire with William and Louis in tow, the small groups of men would stand respectfully at his arrival. These men were veterans of many hard fights, and they looked it. All lean and a bit ragged, they still seemed to carry themselves with an air of professionalism.

William and Louis were congratulated by each group of men for the "great barrel rescue" as everyone was calling it. It was a fine way to be introduced to the company, and the boys liked the attention.

The Captain introduced them to the two lieutenants, his second and third in command. They met all the corporals, and Corporal Heck couldn't resist telling the whole story again to the Captain and his messmates.

After they had made their rounds of A Company, the Captain took them on a tour of the Regimental camp. He had an easy manner, and even though the boys knew he was an officer and their commander, they felt comfortable with him.

"We started this war with six companies of about 100 men each, mostly from Williamson County, with a few Nashville and

Columbia men thrown in. Since all that area is behind the Yankee lines, we obviously haven't been home in over two years. I have a son at home who's much younger than you two." The Captain was quiet for a few minutes as they walked on, deep in reflection.

William and Louis noticed they were heading toward a big tent surrounded by three wagons and several horses and topped off with a big Confederate battle flag on a pole outside the tent. "This is the Regimental Headquarters. We are under the command of Colonel Granville, 2nd Tennessee Cavalry. We're dismounted now, because there just aren't enough horses left in the army, so we fight on foot as infantry. We do a lot of the scouting for General Cleburne's division in General Cheatham's corps, which is made up of two other divisions like General Cleburne's. We're skirmishers, so we are usually spread out in a thin line in front of the infantry regiments, and our job is to find the Yankees so General Cleburne doesn't get surprised, and can then fight them with his main force.

"That's why your jobs are so important. It gets really confusing in a fight. We'll usually be out front spread over a large area, not densely packed like the other regiments. Colonel Granville will be behind us, and when I have something to report to him, I'll send you back to his headquarters. He takes your information and puts it all together with what he's hearing form the other companies and sends his runners back to General Cleburne to decide what to do.

"As you can see, you will play an important role. You will normally give your information to this officer here," the Captain said as they approached another officer with a yellow cap and faded gold braid on his uniform coat.

"Major O'Rourke," Captain Richardson addressed the officer, "I'd like you to meet my two new runners, Private Sweeney and Private Nix. They just joined us yesterday and have already made a name for themselves in the company."

William and Louis stood at attention and saluted the new officer, mimicking what they had seen other soldiers in camp do, and Major O'Rourke returned their salute with a big grin. "I've heard about you already," O'Rourke said. "Which one of you is the cliff jumper?" William blushed and stammered, "Me, Sir."

"Welcome to Granville's Regiment," O'Rourke said, and extended his hand. William shook it, and O'Rourke turned to Captain Richardson, "We just got word from Division that we're heading north soon. Start getting your men ready to move. We cross the river on the pontoon bridge with General Hood on the 13th and, once the whole army is ready, we'll be moving up the Waynesboro Road and then turning east toward Columbia. I'm working on the orders now, and there's a good chance we'll be in the lead with your company up front. You'll be the tip of the sword."

As the two officers began discussing the details, William and Louis were fascinated to listen to the coordination between the regiment and its companies. A few minutes later, Major O'Rourke spoke to the boys. "When you're headed back to me with a message, you watch for this big flag here. See the full moon sewn in the middle? Each unit's flag is a little different, so you watch for this one. I'll be close by. You tell me exactly what Captain Richardson says and remember where you came from so you can get back. Wait by me for a couple of minutes so I can see if I have instructions for you to take back to Captain Richardson, and when I release you, run back to your company. It'll be fast and furious, so make sure I see you and get me your information quickly. Good luck, boys, and again, welcome to the Regiment."

The boys saluted once again, and followed Captain Richardson back to Company A. William was pleased with himself. He had shown the men of the company he was brave and resourceful. He found himself wishing his Pa could be here to see this. He would be proud, he knew, especially with such important work ahead of him. Being a runner sounded exciting, and he pictured himself trotting around the battlefield with important messages, saving the army! What would it be like in battle, he wondered? Would he be brave there, too?

CHAPTER 9
ON THE MOVE

Word of the impending advance started quite a stir back at camp. The weather alternated between Indian summer days and miserable cold rain while they cleaned all the rifles in the wagon and helped Sergeant Ambers get the mules and wagon ready for moving. Henry helped in everything. Every time they thought they had something cleaned and ready, however, First Sergeant Dillard would come over and inspect it and tell them to do it again. Sergeant Ambers took it all in stride, but it upset the boys.

"Don't worry, just do what he says," Sergeant Ambers counseled them. "It keeps us busy and makes you forget that we're going into the fight. You boys take the mules down toward the river and see if you find some grass for them to graze."

The boys led the mules by their halter ropes and watched the Army of Tennessee prepare to advance. All the camps they passed were like their own, busy with organizing and getting their equipment ready to fight. They noticed a lot more wagon traffic as some of the supplies the Army had been waiting on began to arrive.

William noticed that Louis kept asking the teamsters as they passed if they had come up from Mobile or heard anything from down there.

"Your father is down there, ain't he?" William asked when he realized what Louis was doing.

"Yeah," said Louis. "We got a letter from him about a month ago and they was still there in the fort." He turned and looked at William. "I haven't seen him in a long time, but at least he was okay a month ago and I ain't heard nothin' about no big battles down there. I worry about him all the time, thinking maybe he got shipped up here to help out in this fight. You ain't heard nothin' from your Pa in a long time, have you?"

William could feel tears well in his eyes as he thought about his father. He didn't speak. "I know he went to fight for the Yankees, William," Louis said quietly, "but yer' secret's safe with me. Maybe we'll see him as we get closer to Nashville." Louis said this, trying to cheer William up.

"That's what I'm afraid of," William said. "What if I see my Pa and he's across the field shootin' at me? What if I see him get hurt, or I see him walkin' past as a prisoner? What am I gonna' do, Louis?"

Louis thought a minute. "He'll be fine, William." He put his hand on William's shoulder. "He's probably pullin' guard duty up in Indiana, safe as can be, and when this war's over he'll come ridin' back home with a fistful of Yankee dollars. You'll see!"

William just hoped he would see him again, and that they could speak civilly to each other when all this was done.

By the time the boys got back with the mules, Sergeant Ambers had a small fire going and Henry was stirring a pot of cornmeal mush bubbling in the pot. They filled their mess cups, and after they finished eating, Sergeant Ambers announced, "Let's write a letter home."

He produced a weathered piece of paper and small pencil from inside his jacket. William noticed he was writing on the back page of another letter. "I saved up some of these old letters to write home on," when William questioned him about it. "We'll send one letter to Mr. Sims, and he can relay the news to your families.

The three of them drafted their letters:
    To the families of Josiah Ambers, Louis Nix, and William Sweeney
    Fayetteville, Lincoln County, Tennessee
Dear Loved Ones,
    We three are fine, and have arrived safely with the Rebel Army. We are camped on the bank of the Tennessee River and are tolerably well.
    William and Louis are famous already in the company for an adventure getting rations, and help Josiah care for the Company wagon.
    All the boys from Fayetteville made it here safely and we all wish everyone back home well. We will come home safe and we think of ya'll often. You may send to us at Company "A", 2nd Tennessee Cavalry, Army of Tennessee.
                    Your Obedient Servants,
              Josiah, William, and Louis

William noticed Henry looking at them with a longing expression on his face. He looked as homesick as them.

"Henry," William said, "would you like us to write back home to your folks, too?" Henry brightened and said "That'd be nice Mistuh' William, suh. My folks cain't read, but some on'd surely read it to 'em back home!"

Louis ribbed William good for offering. "That's a waste of time, William. How you gonna write a letter for a slave to read back home? Nobody cares what's happened to this boy. He's owned by the army now."

Henry's expression changed immediately, downcast and guarded. His eyes looked moist. William cast a mean glance toward Louis. "That's an awful thing to say, Louis. He's got family back home just like me and you, and they'll want to know he's doin' fine. This alright with you, Sergeant Ambers?"

"Fine by me," and William, Henry and Sergeant Ambers huddled over the new letter while Louis stomped off.

CHAPTER 10

ACROSS THE RIVER

Williams's feet were like blocks of ice. He was cold all over as he awoke to the sounds of the great army shaking itself from slumber and preparing to march, but his feet were especially cold. His blanket was not long enough to cover his whole body, and ended up bunched around his neck every night.

The shoes and socks William wore were pitiful. Both shoes had large holes in the bottom all the way through, and even though William had cut an old cartridge box's leather flap and placed it inside, he could not keep the mud from seeping in and freezing around his feet.

The socks he had found in the wagon were hardly worth calling that. He knew he was lucky, however, as most of the men in the company had no socks at all, and their shoes were just as bad, if not worse than William's. He knew they were going to have to march many days like this, and he shivered even more.

The 2nd Tennessee was moving across the pontoon bridges over the Tennessee with the rest of General Cheatham's corps today – almost 10,000 men. William had watched with interest as the bridges were built from all manner of boats laid side by side and a plank road built across it wide enough for the wagons and cannon to cross. The Tennessee River is wide, and William was a little unsure as to the safety of this crossing, but the veterans assured he and Louis it was better than swimming.

Sergeant Ambers, William and Louis hitched the mules and readied the wagon. Henry folded up the officer's tents and brought them down to the wagon. Soldiers from the company brought over their pitiful tents and meager possessions to load. Sergeant Ambers had received some new rations and ammunition from the commissary two days before and he was checking to make sure it was evenly loaded with the soldier's equipment.

William was disappointed to find out he would not be riding, but would be walking and leading the mules. The mules were really in sad condition and any extra weight would be too much for them. Henry followed in case anything fell off.

The morning was gray and foreboding with dark overcast snow clouds. The wind howled down from the north and whipped right into their faces as the company formed a column behind Captain Richardson and First Sergeant Dillard. Corporal Heck carried the company colors, a smaller version of the regimental flag William had seen at headquarters.

Sixty men in ranks of four abreast made up the body of the unit, followed by William, Louis, and Sergeant Ambers walking with the wagon. Immediately behind them were the other two companies of the 2nd Tennessee. Colonel Granville and his staff led their horses in front of Captain Richardson as the entire regiment wound down the slope to the pontoon bridge.

William could see a continuous line of similar units crossing the bridge, going up the far shore, and behind them as far as he could see. The ground was frozen and he slipped on the crusty ruts left in the road by two weeks of intense wagon and foot traffic. It was terrible on his poor feet, and he hoped he'd get used to it or that the road would get better.

As they approached the bridge they realized that getting the balky mules on it was not going to be easy. The rear rank of soldiers had to help Henry push the wagon, while Sergeant Ambers drove the team and Louis and William pulled them for all they were worth. As they moved father out on the bridge, it began to sway in the current. It made everyone's gait a little unsteady, and the mules had to be driven across.

There were lots of cheers and hurrahs from the men as they reached the far shore. These men were from Tennessee and crossing this river meant they had passed one more big obstacle to getting home. The state line was still twenty miles away, but crossing the river and knowing they were back on the move buoyed their spirits. William and Louis joined the rest in yelling their heads off when they reached the far bank! Much of the Army of Tennessee was made up of Tennessee men, and as each regiment cheered upon reaching the north bank, it became one continuous rolling roar.

General Hood and his staff sat their horses on the north bank and waved their men on. From here on out, Hood knew they had to move fast if they were going to win the race to Columbia. By now, it was known that the Yankees at Pulaski were commanded by General John Schofield. William had even heard that General Hood and General Schofield had been classmates at West Point. Whatever they had been, now they were on a collision course, and William was part of the drama.

General Cheatham rode up to Hood, strapped in his saddle again today. Cheatham did not particularly like Hood, but he had to admire the courage of a man who had already given a leg and an arm to this cause. "Think we can bag them Yankees?" Cheatham asked as he knuckled his forehead in salute.

"Damn right we can," Hood replied. "Look at your boys, General. They've been beat up pretty bad these last few months, but see their spirits! They know they are going home to fight, and that's going to make all the difference. Fightin' on their own soil is worth two divisions. There's nothing they can't do if we lead them right." Cheatham did not reply. Could General Hood really lead them to victory, or just more slaughter?

As it turned out, the men's cheering as they cross the river was a little premature. What with the miserable weather and other delays, it was another week before they actually stepped off on their great adventure.

CHAPTER 11

ROAD MARCH

William marched all day. The heavy rifle he carried and the cartridge box filled with forty rounds of ammunition weighed heavily on his shoulders. All day long, they passed men who had dropped out of the march and the men of the 2nd Tennessee catcalled these stragglers. Even though William's feet were bloody and sore by the end of the day, he was determined to keep up. He noticed that the rags bound around Henry's feet were also beginning to show red with spots of blood. The boys had to push the wagon out of mud holes carved through the icy road many times.

A cheer sounded far ahead down the line of marching men as the sun began to sink in the west. It had begun to spit snow and the trees and grass to their flanks began to take on an icy shimmer. The cheer was almost continuous now, and slowly seemed to roll down the column toward William.

Now the front of the 2nd Tennessee began to cheer and wave their caps. It worked its way back to the wagon and William saw the sign post on the side of the road welcoming the Army of Tennessee back to their namesake state after many battles. It looked homemade and said "Tennessee's a Grave or a Free Home." One year ago these veterans had retreated from Missionary Ridge outside Chattanooga, and been driven out of Tennessee. Now, they were back.

Couriers on horseback moved up and down the column, and just a mile inside the border word came down the line that they were bivouacking for the night. Captain Richardson led them off to the west of the road and trotted back to the wagon, with First Sergeant Dillard in tow.

"Set up camp here, tonight," he told Dillard, "Pull a detail to get some food going and to set up the tents, and I'll get the pickets out. We're the regiments' picket line tonight, half on, half off." The Captain turned to William, "Private Sweeney," he called, "follow me."

As Sergeant Ambers, Louis and Henry began to unload the wagon and unhitch the mules, William trotted behind the Captain as he passed the rest of the company and placed pairs of men in a huge semi-circle facing north at the tree line. William watched the other companies of the 2nd Tennessee doing the same, and then saw the other arriving Regiments move into the middle of the circle and begin to camp.

Once Captain Richardson had his men in place and the picket line established, he sent William running toward Colonel Granville's headquarters to notify him they were in position. It was well after dark by the time William found his way back to Sergeant Ambers and the wagon. Louis had rigged a canvas shelter beside the wagon for the three of them, and Sergeant Ambers had heated up some mush for them to eat. Henry came back from setting up the officer's tents and rigged up a little shelter of his own.

"Well boys," Sergeant Ambers said as he took his last bite, "How did you like your trip to Alabama?"

"It's good to be back home," Louis said. "How far do you think we are from Fayettetown?" Their home was officially named

Fayetteville, but people born and raised around the county still called it Fayettetown from the old days.

"I reckon we're only about sixty miles away right now. I've been down this road from Lawrenceburg, and I say we're about twenty miles away from there and another 20 on to Pulaski, where the Yankees are. Twenty more miles down that road from Pulaski and we're home."

The snow began to fall heavy that night. William thought about his Ma, Becky, and Jim and hoped they were snug inside the farmhouse. He wished he was there. Ma would be singing a soft song to them and Becky and Jim would be playing checkers by the light of the fire in the hearth. Oh, how wonderful that would be right now, he thought.

William's thoughts turned again to Pa. Where was his father? Would he be up this road with the Federal forces? Would he actually have to fight his father in battle? He prayed that his father was safe, and that they would meet again someday in more peaceful times. He took comfort in his mind that his father would have to treat him better now that he was a soldier.

He also had been growing to like Henry, and the thought of having a slave at the farm, someone like Henry who was friendly and a hard worker, began to appeal to William. But he couldn't help thinking that it just didn't seem right that he could own somebody. Maybe his father was right. Forcing someone like Henry to work would be just like his Pa forced him to do things. He knew he hated it. Would Henry hate it too?

William often wondered about the fate of his father. Since they had heard nothing from him, he could only imagine. Perhaps he had been sent to Virginia to fight around Washington. Or, perhaps, he had been sent out to Missouri to garrison one of the many posts out west. Sometimes he thought his father must have been killed long ago, soon after he left, and lay buried on one of hundreds of bloody fields scattered around the country that cradled fallen men. When William dreamed of his father lying dead on some forgotten field, he always woke up crying.

Now that William was living the life of a soldier, it seemed to bring him closer to his father. Perhaps his dad was sleeping out in the cold and snowy night looking up at the same sky as he. William hoped he was warm and safe and dry wherever he was, and wished again they would be reunited soon.

Well before dawn First Sergeant Dillard strode by, cursing and yelling at them to wake up and pack the wagon. William shook the snow off his blanket where it had blown in and elbowed Louis, dozing next to him.

Louis woke with a start and called out "Mama! Mama!" He looked around glassy eyed and took a minute to focus on William's face. "I was dreaming of home," he finally said as he began to unbundle. In the night Louis had piled everything he could find on himself. The two mule blankets, a scrap of canvas, even the lid to an empty cracker tin, all lay piled on top of him.

"Lordy, Louis, you look like a gypsy," William said grinning.

"I'm freezing to death, William," Louis said through chattering teeth. "Help me get this stuff off."

Sergeant Ambers stuck his head under the ragged canvas, "Come on, boys, get moving. You two hitch up those mules quiet now and I'll try to heat us up some breakfast."

Henry awoke too, and said good morning to the three of them, and then shuffled off to get the fire going at the officer's tent and heat up their breakfast.

"We'll save you some, Henry," William called to his back, and Henry turned and nodded thanks.

"He ain't getting' none of mine," Louis murmured.

Sergeant Ambers stirred the coals of their cook fire from last night after brushing off the snow. He got a small spark going and within minutes had a fire under a pot of water. He threw in some of the corn meal and cut off a small chunk of dried beef they had been issued as they rolled out of Florence yesterday.

The company moved about them doing the same thing. As William draped the tack over the first mule's head he saw Captain Richardson moving quietly between the small campfires talking to his men. William liked Captain Richardson. He seemed an educated, well-respected man, and his quiet competence and easy manner with the troops made William confident.

"We ought to name the mules," Louis broke his thoughts. "Let's name one Miss Lucinda after our school teacher, and the other Becky, after your sister."

"I'm not naming no mule after my sister!" William said. "I can just see her face when I get home and tell her my mule was named Becky. She'd be mad as a hornet!"

"How 'bout Old Abe," said Louis as he pulled an empty pail out of the wagon. Old Abe, it is," said William. "Now get some water for the mules, or Miss Lucinda and Old Abe will be ornery than ever today."

The Company was on the march as the sun peaked over the horizon. The weather was still awful, but the frozen ground was better that moving through mud. The fields were coated with a blanket of light snow, and it gave everything a clean look that was pleasant to William.

He could see the dark shapes of Cavalrymen out on the flanks now, shadowing the column of men moving north. "Who are those riders, Sergeant Ambers?" he asked as they trudged along side by side. Sergeant Ambers had let Henry drive the team for awhile since his feet looked so bad.

"They are our cavalry, and now that we're moving deep into Tennessee they are scouting and watching for ambushers. You can bet there's a whole mess of our cavalry out looking for Yankees right now. Talk is we're trying to head off a Yank army about our size over toward Pulaski before they can hook up with the Yanks in Nashville."

William always thought of his Pa when someone talked of Yankees.

"Worried about your Pa, William?" Sergeant Ambers asked quietly. "Someday, this war will be over and if the Lord wills it, he'll be back home safe." Sergeant Ambers, of course, knew about William's father.

"I heard what your Pa did to get those Lincoln County boys back after Shiloh. It was a brave thing to do and it gave comfort to a lot of folks around home. No one holds anything against him for fighting for the Yanks; he was just in the wrong place at the wrong time. For folks like us, William, we mostly just want to be left alone. Sure I signed up early, but mostly just to get out of the county and see some adventure." He waggled his empty shirt-sleeve. "Some adventure," he said wryly.

"Thanks for lookin' out for Louis and me," William said. "Gettin' back here in this wagon may save our lives. I've got to get back home in one piece, no offense." He looked at Sergeant Amber's empty jacket sleeve. "Cause Ma and the kids need me. We've got food stored for winter and lots of wood cut, but when Spring comes …" William's voice trailed off as he thought about his Ma and Becky and Jim trying to get the crop in the ground without him.

They marched on north until noon and then turned to the east. By noon the next day they had struck the Columbia Pike at Mount Pleasant. Now the Confederate column was moving through some of the most beautiful countryside in the South. The farms they passed impressed William, and as they finally marched off the turnpike to bivouac, he noticed the blazing lights of torches and campfires already burning by a large mansion.

"That's Ashwood," Captain Richardson told them as they set up the wagon and issued out the ragged tents to the Company. "It was built by the late General Polk, who was killed in Georgia back in the summer, but some years ago, he sold it to his brother Andrew. It's quite a grand place. As a younger man, I rode by here several times. General Hood will probably be staying there for a day or two."

CHAPTER 12
ASHWOOD

Music floated over the fields from the big house at Ashwood that evening while, across the road, magnificent Saint John's Church stood solemn and silent in the moonlight. General Schofield was withdrawing his army out of town and across the Duck River, and much of the Columbia Gentry had come down to meet General Hood and welcome their liberators. Once William and Louis had taken care of the mules, and heard Sergeant Ambers snoring, they snuck out of camp and walked over to the edge of the light.

Fine carriages and beautiful horses were tied up outside the house. Men in tall hats and ladies in fine dresses could be seen socializing with the officers around the mansion, and a band played dances and martial tunes for the crowd.

William and Louis were not alone in watching the festivities. They joined a throng of men standing around the fringes of the party. An older soldier pointed out some of the dignitaries.

"That's General Cheatham there, and there's General Hood," someone said, and William recognized the officer who had raised a cheer for him back on the Tennessee River,

"Here comes Governor Harris, and Bishop Quintard's with him," the man said excitedly as another carriage came into view.

From several arriving wagons large quantities of food were brought out and laid on hastily set up tables. William had not seen a spread like that since before the war at the county fairs. He could hear Louis's stomach growl, and was sure his was also audible.

"We need to sneak in there and get some of them vittles," the older soldier near them said in a whisper.

"Here's our plan: you two stand at attention and follow my orders. I'll march you right up to the Governor's carriage like I'm placing a detail on it. You two stand guard at the horses' head and at the back of the wagon.

"We don't know how to march or do any of that," Louis protested. "We've only been here a few weeks."

"Don't worry, don't worry, the older man said. "You just march in step; you can do that easy enough, and hold your rifles out at port arms, like this." He showed the boys how to do that. "When I say "Order Arms," you snap your rifles butt ends down on the ground and stand stock still. I'll do all the talkin'. One of those fine civilian ladies will see how young you two are and she'll bring you some vittles. You keep standin' at attention like, and I'll say you're on guard duty and I'll take it for you. Then when she's gone, we'll march back over here and split it up. What do you say?"

William and Louis looked at each other and listened to their stomachs growl. They grinned at the same time and snapped to attention. The older soldier adjusted their cartridge belts and ragged uniform coats, tilted their caps down at perfect angles, and commanded "Forward March!" He walked ahead of them right up to the finest carriage in the yard.

"Detail, halt!" he cried. "Move to your posts!" he commanded, and in perfect order, William and Louis moved to their assigned locations. Even though it was still very cool, nervous perspiration dripped down William's face. They watched as the soldier marched to the back of the carriage facing the house, and in perfect parade ground voice, called "Order Arms!" The boys snapped their rifles to the ground and stood stock-still.

Sure enough, the little detail had attracted some attention at the house. The Governor turned briefly to watch the special guard on his carriage, and William heard him thank the officer he was speaking to for the consideration.

Just then, another large carriage arrived, and to William's astonishment, it was filled with pretty girls! Although most of them were older than William, and there was an older lady who must have been their chaperone, one looked to be about his age, and she was the prettiest girl he had ever seen. Her cherubic face was fringed in blonde ringlets, and her eyes flashed in the firelight. He felt his face glow red as her eyes fell on him.

As the young ladies walked by, William couldn't take his eyes off the little blonde – and then she winked at him! William couldn't believe it. He wasn't sure he really saw it, but she sure seemed to have winked at him. His heart soared, but he stood at a rigid attention. So did Louis and the other soldier, as was their plan, but William hadn't counted on this!

The Governor and a lady who seemed to be the hostess greeted the group and they all moved inside the big house, and William's heart sank as the girl disappeared from sight.

"Patience boys, patience," the old soldier said under his breath. We're in. They've seen us and it won't be long now. Just hold your spot, and keep your knees bent a little so you don't pass out."

About thirty minutes later, William's heart leapt into his throat when an officer approached the older soldier.

"How're you men doing, soldier?" he asked.

"Fine, sir. Guard detail, sir," came the old soldier's reply.

"Carry on. Fine job, men," and the officer walked away.

William let out a huge sigh as he left. What would happen to him if First Sergeant Dillard found out his ruse? Just as Dillard's horrible countenance filled his thoughts, the young girl he had seen stepped out onto the porch alone. She looked around and then let her gaze stop on William. He again caught his breath. His knees locked and he felt the pounding of his heart every second.

She seemed to stand there watching him forever. Then she turned on her heels as if she had just made her mind up about something and disappeared back into the mansion.

A few minutes later she reappeared carrying a small bundle in a dainty lace handkerchief. She lightly strode down the steps and seemed to glide over to the carriage. The old soldier snapped to attention, and said "Evening, Miss," as she approached.

"Thank you men for watching over the carriages," she said in a sweet voice. I thought you looked famished, so I brought you some treats from the house. I know it was probably foolish of me, but I just couldn't bear the thought of you men going hungry out here protecting us. It's been so long since I've seen a real Southern gentleman." She spoke to the soldier, but her eyes were on William.

"Thank you, Miss," the soldier said as he took the bundle from her. "I'll see the young lads get this." "Thank you, sir" she said, and moved toward the horse where William was standing.

"She's a wonderful animal," she casually said to William as she approached.

"Yes, Miss, a wonderful animal," William said as he stood ramrod straight in his best soldier pose. She took off her glove and reached into a hidden pocket in her skirt and pulled out a cube that she fed to the horse. William's mouth watered for the sugar she had just fed the animal.

"Do you know horses?" she asked. "Yes, miss, he said, in his deepest voice, which promptly cracked. She smiled. "I've brought you a special treat from inside," she said and slipped another small package into his coat pocket. William could not move. He was absolutely frozen solid. He could feel his heart pounding. Then she leaned up and kissed him on his cheek.

"Be brave in the coming battle," she said, and quickly turned back towards the house just as the older woman stepped out on the porch to look for her. In another moment, she was gone.

The old soldier turned his head slowly and gave William a mischievous grin. After that, William would have stood by that horse and carriage until Hell froze over.

An hour later, Williams's legs were aching. He had marched over terrible roads for three days and his legs were worn out. He was cold, and was dying to know what she had put in his jacket, but he dared not move.

The party was breaking up, and the Governor and Bishop Quintard and the young ladies were among the first to leave. As they descended the steps, William noticed to his horror an officer accompanying them that he immediately recognized: Captain Richardson. The Captain escorted the ladies to the carriage while the Governor and the Bishop said their goodbyes to the Generals. As Captain Richardson got closer, William debated on whether to run for it. He was not supposed to be here, and he and Louis were going to get caught and he didn't know what would happen to him. He stood stock still, and tried to let his cap cover his face.

"Goodbye, my dear Mrs. Warfield," Captain Richardson said to the older woman as they approached.

"Goodnight John," the lady said as he helped her into the carriage. Just then, the young girl walked by, so close to William that he could smell her sweet perfume. She brushed her skirt past him and turned back to Captain Richardson.

"Goodnight, cousin," she said, and kissed the captain just inches away from William's face. Captain Richardson accepted her kiss, and then turned to see William standing there scared to death. Emotion played across his face; recognition, surprise, and then a conspiratorial smile.

"Goodnight, Cousin Mattie," the Captain said.

CHAPTER 13

THE ELEPHANT

Captain Richardson returned to the party after chastising William and Louis. The boys split the treats with the old soldier and slinked back to camp. They dreaded the next morning but were glad the captain had not publicly humiliated them in front of the ladies.

William's special gift from the girl was a piece of sweet cake, and he and Louis savored every bite, but William's most cherished possession now was the lace handkerchief she had used to wrap the cake. It was wonderful, and its delicateness enthralled him.

The next morning he awoke to First Sergeant Dillard's boot.

"Get up, you rotten boys!" Dillard yelled. "What do you mean leaving my camp? Don't you know you don't pass water without my say so?"

William and Louis took their scolding. Secretly, they decided the sweet cake was worth it. First Sergeant Dillard worked them harder than ever that morning, and by noon they were exhausted. The weather had turned a little warmer and the sun shone down on them. Late that afternoon, Captain Richardson came back from a meeting at headquarters and called the company together.

"Tomorrow's the fight, men," he began. "The whole Yankee army is just on the other side of the river. General Forrest is scaring off their cavalry now. Some of our boys are going to hold them there in the morning while we march around behind and hit them in the backside. We'll be crossing the river on a pontoon bridge that's gonna be built tonight, so the wagon will stay here. Once across, we'll be in enemy territory, but Forrest's cavalry will be somewhere out in front of us, so watch before you fire at anything. General Cleburne's division will be in the lead, with our regiment out front, as usual, so travel light and make sure your cartridge box is full."

"We'll support Forrest and be the hammer that breaks the Yankee route of retreat back to Nashville. No straggling tomorrow, men. We're going to bag the lot of them and we need every rifle."

That evening, as the men were cooking some extra rations to carry with them and making final checks of their gear, Captain Richardson walked over to the wagon. "Sergeant Ambers, you'll be on your own tomorrow," he said. "You corral with the rest of the teamsters and we'll probably meet you on the road north of Columbia. Keep Henry with you. He can be your right hand"

He then turned to the boys with a slight grin on his face. "Well, little gentlemen, after your escapade last night, are you ready to do some real soldiering?"

"Yes, sir!" they answered in unison.

"It'll be a long day tomorrow, so try to get some sleep. You two will be with me at the head of the column, and you'll see the elephant before sundown," referring to the term used for combat. "Make sure they're ready, Sergeant Ambers." He turned and walked back to the company.

"You sure got yourselves in a fine mess last night," Sergeant Ambers said. He too suppressed a smile. William had shared their treats with Sergeant Ambers, so he knew the whole story.

"Make sure your cartridge boxes are full, fill your canteens, and pack a little hard tack in your haversack. You got caps?" he asked, referring to the little percussion caps required to fire their rifles.

"Yes, Sergeant," they said. William packed some extra straw in his shoes to help cushion his feet from the road. "See you boys by tomorrow night, I hope, and you keep your heads down. I don't want to have to tell your mamas any sad stories when I get home!"

It was still dark when William and Louis slung their rifles and joined the Captain at the head of the column the next morning. They flanked Corporal Heck with the colors and watched the regiment, and then the entire division form up. As they headed north, they heard the booming of artillery off to their left toward General Stephen Lee's corps. Most of the Army's artillery had been left with Lee to demonstrate in front of the Yankees at Columbia. His job was to keep the Yankees distracted so the rest of the Confederate Army could circle around behind them.

Company A was the first of the infantry to cross the pontoon bridge over the Duck River, just after dawn. It was going to be a beautiful day for William's first battle. Very soon, however, the country lanes turned muddy with the passage of marching men, and the going was rough, but William felt their spirits were high. Hour after hour, they marched north.

Finally, in the middle of the afternoon, they came to a small creek, but they rolled up their pants legs, took off their shoes and kept moving. A big cavalryman sat on his horse as they came up the opposite bank and directed General Govan, their brigade commander, to move quietly from here on out. In the distance, off to the left, a fine big house sat on a little rise.

"The Federals are a mile or so up the road at a little town of Spring Hill," William heard the cavalryman say to the officers at the head of the column. He watched excitedly as the message was relayed to the 2nd Tennessee's regimental commander, Colonel

Granville, and then down to Captain Richardson. Even General Hood and General Cleburne and some staff officers rode up while this discussion was going on. William felt he was witnessing history in the making.

After the officer's meeting ended, a guide on horseback led Captain Richardson and A Company on down the road, with B Company and the rest of the regiment close on their heels. After they had gone maybe half a mile, they were turned off the road to the left, near a small hill. Just then, a runner came from Colonel Granville, and William heard him tell Captain Richardson to establish a skirmish line at the top of the rise and wait for the rest of the division to form behind them.

All around William, the men began efficiently taking most of the rails off the split rail fence along the road and laying them on the ground. William helped but wondered why this was necessary. "We take these down so the regular infantry regiments coming up behind us can maneuver through them," said Corporal Heck when William looked at him quizzically. Everything about this seemed strange to William who had spent his whole life trying to keep fences repaired.

As Captain Richardson directed his company off the left side of the road and up the small rise, B Company began to fan out, extending the line to the right as the rest of the regiment came up the road. William stuck close to the Captain in the center as did Louis, Corporal Heck, and First Sergeant Dillard, while the two lieutenants had charge of the men of A Company on either flank.

"Private Sweeney," the Captain said as he looked at the boys. "Keep your eyes on Lieutenant Jones on the left. Private Nix, you watch Lieutenant Dunn on the right. If I have a message for them, you run straight there and then back to me at the colors." The company moved forward, rifles at the ready, until they were near the crest of the little rise. As they reached the top, William could suddenly see a large field stretched out in front of him. Judging

Confederate Winter

from the old corn stalks crunching beneath the men's feet, this farmer had made a good crop that year.

All day long, William had heard the officers talking about the road to Nashville and how they were going to take it and trap the Yankees. Now, Captain Richardson called William and Louis to him and pointed to the far edge of the field, over a mile away. "Look close and you can see the Pike through the breaks in the woods over there. General Forrest has some of the Yankees cooped up in the town up on that far hill to the right, but a lot more are still trying to get here from Columbia. General Cleburne's been ordered to march over there and block the Pike, so our job will be to stay out front and make sure the division doesn't get surprised." Sure enough, William could just see a thin line in a few places at the far edge that had to be the road, but the field in front of him looked completely empty. If they were going into battle, where was the enemy? Suddenly William actually felt a little disappointed. This was going to be too easy. William very soon found out that he had a lot to learn about war.

For the moment, however, there was nothing for William to do, so he looked back towards the road and watched as the division arrived. General Cleburne had over three thousand men divided into three brigades, and as he watched them form up, William began to feel like a real soldier.

A few minutes later, runners came from Colonel Granville to Captain Richardson and the other company commanders and the line of skirmishers was told to advance about two hundred yards to give the division more room. William kept his eye on Lieutenant Jones to his left. He was about fifty yards away, and the steadily moving line of men extended from him, past William, all the way down to a strip of timber lining the right edge of the large field. William could see the regimental infantry deploy behind them in columns from the road and out into the fields, flags waving at their fronts. Behind them more men poured out from the trees down by the creek crossing. Most of the regiments' colors carried the distinctive full moon insignia of General Cleburne's division.

Out in front of them, the Pike was still a mile away at least, but William could begin to make out a wagon or two and a few riders on it now. He had to shade his eye to see them clearly, because the sun was dropping lower in the sky just to William's left.

Colonel Granville came riding up to Captain Richardson and pointed with his sword to the right, toward the town. "Forrest says the Yanks are dug in on a hill beyond that line of timber and across a little creek. The brigades will be formed in a few minutes and then General Cleburne is going to throw the whole division across the Pike there in front of us. Once we're there, the Yanks will never move us, and we'll have their army cut in two. Watch my flag for the signal to advance. We don't want any mistakes today."

"Private Sweeney, run to Lieutenant Jones and tell him what you just heard the Colonel say and tell him to keep his eyes on me!" Louis was sent to Lieutenant Dunn with the same message. His first orders! William took off across the field, but the stubble from the old crop was higher and thicker here, so his rifle kept catching on the old stalks and briars tangled his feet as he went. He was running close behind the line of men, and they called to him as he struggled through the brambles. "Run, William! Run! Bring me back some sweet cake!" and the like. Obviously, the men in the company had heard about his adventures at the party.

William reached Lieutenant Jones and relayed the message, then hurried back to the Captain. Louis came back, panting and out of breath, a minute or two later. William was beginning to appreciate all that farm work and plowing that had given him his strong legs. A mile or so to their front, across the big open field, lay the Nashville Pike, visible in a few spots between small stands of timber. Off to the right, beyond the line of trees where Colonel Granville had pointed his sword, William guessed, was the little town of Spring Hill. But where were the Yankees, he wondered?

He could feel perspiration form in the small of his back. His senses seemed sharper than ever. He watched a hawk circle lazily overhead.

Along with Captain Richardson, William now turned to look back for Colonel Granville's flag and watch as the last brigade fell into line. It was awesome to see the full power of a division of infantry arrayed there in front of them.

As they viewed the spectacle, Captain Richardson nonchalantly said to William, "I see you met my cousin Mattie while on your so called guard detail. She seemed to take a shine to you."

"What?" William said, taken aback at the captain's train of thought. He quickly added, "S-Sir?" He couldn't believe the captain was so calm as to discuss this with all the tension building.

"Rumor has it, she brought you sweet cakes that night. Were they good?"

"E-excellent, Sir" William stammered again. The sight of 3,000 men moving in unison was overpowering, but he tried to concentrate on what the captain was saying. Louis and Heck grinned at his discomfort, and First Sergeant Dillard glowered at him.

"Mattie's a sweet girl. She's a student at The Athenaeum, a very fine school for young ladies in Columbia, but classes have been suspended because of the fighting. The school has arranged transportation and General Schofield has granted safe passage to Nashville for the boarding students who wish to go home. Mattie told me that they were leaving yesterday, and she will ride with them as far as Franklin. She was so happy that she and some of the other girls who had relatives in the Army were allowed to attend the ball at Ashwood. Mrs. Warfield, the Headmaster's wife, was the older lady you saw with them. Such beautiful young creatures could not be allowed to travel unescorted." The captain smiled mischievously at William's obvious embarrassment. "Well, when all this is over, I'll have to properly introduce you two. God willing, Mattie should already be safely home."

By now, the division was fully deployed behind them. General Cleburne rode out in front, and, raising his sword, pointed due west to the setting sun. William could not hear what he said, but his martial manner indicated the assault was on. Colonel Granville's flag waved and Captain Richardson yelled, "On the other side of this field, men, lies the Nashville Pike. Capture that road boys, and we cut off the Yankees and win the day. To your duty, Company A!"

The air was electric with excitement. The cannons had been left behind at Columbia, and their continuous booming in the distance indicated they were engaged, keeping the Federals pinned down to the south. William walked beside Corporal Heck who carried the Company guidon, which flapped lightly in the cool breeze. The 60 men of A Company walked slowly out in front of the two lines of the regiment to their rear about a hundred yards. William checked his rifle's percussion cap and carried it at the ready, as if he were hunting squirrels. The thin line of advancing men just in front of him provided some small degree of comfort.

They moved like this for about another 400 yards when William began to hear the crack of rifles. He could see small puffs coming from the tree line to his right, and he immediately thought of his father. Could his Dad be among those Yankees in the trees, firing at his own son?

William could see General Cleburne and his staff from where he was, moving with the advancing men. He could see the skirmishers at the right end of the field begin to stop and fire, then reload. As the Confederates kept advancing, the firing from the trees grew heavier and heavier.

Now, he could begin to see Union flags and a line of breastworks at the edge of the woods they approached. He saw Yankee skirmishers out in front fire and run back to the safety of this line. There didn't seem to be any firing in front of him, but as the right side of the Confederate line advanced, the firing down there got heavier and heavier.

"No artillery yet," said Captain Richardson to First Sergeant Dillard and the men around him.

"Fine with me, Cap'n," Dillard called back.

Just as the words left his mouth, from off to the right front, came the loud booms of firing cannons. William saw huge billows of smoke and flame erupting from them, and a split second later heard their massive reports. It was the loudest noise he had ever known. He witnessed several explosions between the 2nd Tennessee and the following regiment, just as he heard the shriek of the shells racing through the air. It was horrendous. It seemed as if all the men flinched at once, but they kept moving, crouching low.

The firing was really heavy now off to the right, and as the smoke drifted towards him it began to envelop the Confederate formation. As the brigade on the right turned to face the Yankees in the tree line head on, William began to see the middle brigade swing around to line up with them and feel his own brigade being dragged along too. He had a fleeting thought that they were being pulled away from the pike, but then the developing battle took over his full attention. As Company A, on the far end away from the woods, struggled to swing around in a big arc towards the fighting, William saw the rest of the skirmishers in front of the Confederate division begin to stop and fire at the Federals. For the first time, William heard a new sound as rifle balls now began to whistle in the air around him.

More massive shots from the cannon billowed and then roared in his ears. William's attention was focused on keeping an eye on Lieutenant Jones way over on the left, but he saw another shell explode harmlessly behind him. It threw up a great spray of dirt and dust, and seconds later the regiment behind them marched into the cloud and through it.

Captain Richardson had stopped the company about four hundred yards from the Union position, and since his men were veterans they kept up a continuous fire. The two ranks behind them were closing the gap fast now, methodically moving forward.

The next volley of cannon fire came quick and tore great gaps in the advancing Confederates. William even saw one of the 2nd Tennessee men fall to the ground. The roar of battle had completely engulfed him and his eyes looked around wildly. Run! His brain shot this command through every fiber of his being. Just as he turned to obey, he noticed to his amazement Captain Richardson, First Sergeant Dillard, and Corporal Heck seemed calm as could be. Louis on the other hand, also looked like a frightened deer ready to bolt. The sound and fury were overwhelming.

Twenty yards, now ten. The regiment behind moved past William and his little group. Captain Richardson turned and actually grinned as they moved past him. Two big, bearded men passed William, looking grim. At the skirmish line the two marching files stopped as one, and without any orders at all, the front rank fired in unison and the whole world was engulfed in smoke.

William felt the heat from the volley blow back in his face as the Confederate's next rank fired. A tremendous blast of hot air whipped past William's left side, and he saw two men stagger out of the rifle smoke and fall within feet of him. Still another volley rang out from his front, followed by another, a little more ragged this time. And then the regiment moved past and left the 2nd Tennessee behind. William could see gaps in their line even through the smoke and confusion, and noticed bundles of rags laying in heaps to his left.

"Runners!" Captain Richardson yelled. William and Louis moved up to his side so they could hear their instructions. "We are turning oblique back to the west to protect the flank. Execute now! Say it back to me!" The Captain had to yell at them at the top of his lungs to make himself heard.

Neither William nor Louis had ever heard the word "oblique," so the captain had to repeat himself a couple of times. The boys ran off in opposite directions, William wildly searching for Lieutenant Jones. He stumbled over one of the fallen men. The 2nd Tennessee's skirmish line was kneeling now, rifles at the ready, and in just a moment, William was at Jones's side. He relayed the command and sprinted back to Captain Richardson using Corporal Heck's guidon as his guide. Louis returned moments later.

The battle was raging to their front and right. Smoke blew back on them so they could only see shadows and hear the loud reports of cannon and rifle fire. It was no longer in volleys, just the continuous roar of fighting, with men occasionally staggering back through the smoke.

Captain Richardson and the First Sergeant had the middle of the line ready, and William followed Corporal Heck as they moved left away from the fighting. In moments the whole line was moving, and within a hundred yards, they were out of the smoke and facing southwest, back towards the pike and covering the left flank of the battle. No one faced them, and their right flank disappeared into the battle smoke. There they waited, watching that critical sector of the field for approaching Federal troops. The sun was very low on the horizon and parts of the field were deep in shadow.

The sun sank below the horizon and began to plunge the battle into darkness, stabbing flames of firing showing the lines of the two armies. As total darkness fell, there was an undeniable lowering of the sounds of battle as the soldiers disengaged. A rider approached Captain Richardson. It was Colonel Granville. He spoke briefly with the captain and once again William was sent off to Lieutenant Jones. His instructions this time were to bed down where they were, but to keep a picket out and be alert for friendly troops moving up from the south. Another of General Cheatham's division was down there and would try to link up with Cleburne's men.

The men were exhausted and collapsed where they were, but William could see they were still vigilant for a counter-attack. The two lieutenants came back and sat with Captain Richardson to discuss the assault. William listened as Captain Richardson repeated what he had been told.

"The Colonel says our right flank got stung pretty good. We flushed the Federals out of the woods, though, and across that little creek, but then they fell back into a line of breastworks on top of a hill over there and we could not get at them. General Cleburne was up so close that his horse got wounded. Since the Yankees pulled us around to the north, it also means that we have not secured the road. Everyone thinks we need to get over there to cut Schofield's army off in Columbia, but so far we have no orders. We're going to rest here for an hour or so, and then, if General Bate's boys haven't shown up, we'll send out a patrol to find them and bring them in. In the meantime, I want to know what's going on out on the pike."

The captain pointed at Lieutenant Jones. "Give your boys half an hour to rest and get a bite to eat, and then take twenty men and see how far you can go towards the pike. Take Private Sweeney here with you to get your report back to me."

Lieutenant Jones and William moved off into the darkness. The stars were out and it was clear, so they had little trouble finding their way. Small fires were already being started as the men cooked their meager rations. Someone handed William a cup of what passed for coffee in the Confederate Army, and he watched while the lieutenant picked 20 men and briefed them on the night's patrol.

Half an hour later, they stepped off into the darkness. Two men lead the way, two men walked on either flank, and the rest moved in single file behind the lieutenant. William stuck very close to Lieutenant Jones. On their right they could see the campfires of the Federals twinkling in the distance.

One hundred yards out and nothing. Two hundred, then five hundred. William felt they were well past the day's battle line, and even though they were heading due west, away from the carnage, William was tense, fearing they would run into the Federals. As they reached the woods on the far side of the field, the little band halted and listened intently. Nothing.

The lieutenant stationed two men there to guide them back and watch their rear. He didn't want to come back and discover Yankees had occupied this ground without some advance warning.

They moved out again quietly, heading deeper into the brush. Every snapping twig and crunching leaf seemed to reverberate though the night, signaling their approach. William sweated with the strain and concentration. He followed Lieutenant Jones as closely as he could, gaining strength from the proximity of the officer.

The foliage grew denser and a front of clouds came in from the north and began to block some of the light from the moon. It got harder and harder to see in the inky darkness, and William strained to see Lieutenant Jones to his front. He finally moved by sound alone.

A brilliant flash lit the night just off to their right, followed by the crack of a rifle, then another. William felt, more than saw, Lieutenant Jones drop in front of him as they all tried to figure out what was happening. They heard voices and the sound of someone running toward them as more shots were fired. The two men covering the right came crashing through the underbrush, and more shots ripped through the leaves over their heads. William distinctly heard the thud of a ball striking something solid above his head.

More firing now, and Lieutenant Jones's little band began to fire back. Each muzzle flash seemed to destroy William's night vision.

A fist grabbed William by the jacket, and Lieutenant Jones's face pressed against his ear. "Sweeney, go back and tell the captain we've run into the Yankees about 200 yards into the tree line. Tell him we're coming back in. Be quick, boy!" More shots rang out, and William groped through the darkness, back toward the company and safety. He had to get back and let the captain know what was going on.

The firing intensified behind him and he moved faster through the scrub. His forehead struck something with a crack, and he felt himself knocked backwards onto the ground. Stars swirled in front of his eyes and he blacked out momentarily. As he stood up, he noticed that all the firing had stopped and it was dead quiet again. He ran through the forest for a minute or two, breathing hard, before he realized he was disoriented.

The moon was completely covered by clouds now, and all the dense growth looked the same to him. He was not sure which way to go and he felt weak and vulnerable. He kept moving, hoping to run into the two men left at the edge of the clearing. They had to be just up ahead.

Fifteen minutes later William knew he was lost. He should have been back at the field by now. He heard nothing but his own breathing and was too deep in the thicket to see any of the campfires.

He followed a ravine that he hoped would lead him back east toward the Confederate lines. At least if he ran into trouble he had a place to hide. He now crept slower and slower and worked his way along, rifle at the ready. He dared not call out for Lieutenant Jones because he could be right in the middle of the Yankee line for all he knew. But he had to get the message back, so he kept moving.

The pines began to thin and he could see an opening ahead of him. This had to be the right way, so he moved cautiously and peered into the blackness. He could not see far, but he heard nothing threatening.

He took a deep breath and exhaled slowly, figuring out what to do. He decided to keep going and hoped this was the field the company occupied. He had to be careful or one of the Confederate sentries might shoot him as he came back through the line. His head hurt, and he felt something wet drip into his right eye.

William continued to hug the little ravine, even though it was clear of brush. Out in the open, he felt much more exposed, but anything was better than crashing around in the thickets. At least he could be quieter as he moved.

When William stepped out of the brush and walked up on the Nashville Pike he knew his navigation had gone terribly wrong. He knew it was the pike because it was a big, wide road, not the farm trail they had taken that morning. William also knew he was probably behind the Yankee line and a long way from safety.

From his left, he heard the sound of marching men. Could the Yankee troops be moving up this road right now, with William standing in the middle of it? How bad could his luck be tonight?

He leapt down into a ditch that ran parallel to the road, only a few feet from the pike. As he huddled there, not daring to breathe, he heard the marching men grow closer. Soon an entire column of men was moving down the Pike, almost on top of him.

He knew immediately they were Federals. They wore boots and shoes that made a distinctive noise as they struck the packed earth. William had been with the Confederate Army long enough to know that the Rebels moved much quieter, primarily because so many had no shoes. The Rebels sounded more padded when they marched, and William knew right away the Yankees were on the move. He had to get this information to Captain Richardson. He'd know what to do!

Men kept moving past him. He heard the rumble as an artillery piece went by, and the jingle of several officers on horseback. When he perceived a gap in the column, he slowly started to creep out of the ditch toward the woods. "Halt! Who goes there?" shouted a Northern voice out of the darkness. Somebody had seen him!

William ran. He ran as fast and as hard as he could go. He ran right out of the sorry excuse for shoes he was wearing, and reached the tree-line as a shot rang out behind him. He didn't stop at all, just plunged ahead. He had his bearings now – the Yankees had to be marching north - and he really had an important mission. He had to get this news back! Now that he felt his direction was right, he did his best to head straight as an arrow east. He knew he'd eventually have to run into Confederates, and he could relay the news.

He made it through the woods and was back in another huge field. There was no sign of Lieutenant Jones, but he could now easily see the flickering campfires of the Rebel army, and also see the Federal lines to his left toward Spring Hill. He now had to watch carefully for Confederate pickets.

He spotted a torch light in the distance on a small hill and decided that had to be the mansion they passed that morning. It became his guide. If he could get there he could find his way back to Captain Richardson. When the sentry challenged him out of the darkness, William was never so happy to hear a Southern drawl!

"It's me! Private Sweeney!" he called back. "2nd Tennessee." The sentry took him into the lines and back to a Major from some regiment he didn't recognize.

When the Major heard William's story, he said, "We've got to get you back to General Hood. If he knows the Yanks are on the move, he'll get us pushing tonight."

The Major went with William up to the mansion which was General Hood's headquarters' for the night. William heard the Major explaining to General Hood's staff officer on duty what William had seen.

"Wait here, I'll wake the General," the officer said, and went inside. A few moments later he came back for them. "Go in soldier, and tell the General what you saw. Be brief, it's been a hard day and the General's not well."

As William went in the lit entryway, he saw himself in a full length mirror in the hall, and he was a mess. No shoes or socks, and his feet left blood stains on the carpet. His trousers were in tatters from the brambles in the woods, and he was covered in mud from the ditch. His sorry-looking, blood-stained hand-me-down jacket was just as bad. His face was filthy and his eyes were sunken and bloodshot. His hair hung down from under his disheveled cap like wet string. General Hood wouldn't listen to a poor looking soul like him.

The staff officer motioned him to a door. "The General will see you now," and with that William walked in and snapped to attention.

General Hood lay wrapped in a blanket on the couch. His wooden log stood beside him. He opened his eyes and tried to focus on William over his big bushy beard. He looked sick.

"Report, Private," he said casually. William told him his story, and he saw the fire come alive in General Hood's eyes.

"You saw none of our troops blocking the road?" General Hood asked.

"None Sir," William said. "Not until I got almost here."

"Good job, son. What unit?" "2nd Tennessee, Sir," William said. "I'll make sure your Captain hears about this. Dismissed."

As William left the room, he saw General Hood struggle to a seated position with his good arm, and heard him shouting for his staff officers.

The energy drained from William like sap from a tree. He walked out into the yard, stumbled to a small tree, and collapsed. He slept like the dead.

CHAPTER 14

ALMOST HOME

The courier galloped into the front yard of the house and just missed trampling William.

"They're gone General! They're gone! The Yankees have pulled out in the night. We missed them sir!"

William struggled to his feet and the courier tossed him the reins and ran up the steps into the house. Other officers, half dressed, also ran to the house. William could hear General Hood haranguing men around him and cursing in unbridled frustration. The sun just began to wink over the horizon.

"The best maneuver of my life, wasted! How did they escape?! How did they get by us? We should have crushed them today. Why wasn't the road blocked?" General Hood cried.

No one could answer him.

"When we catch those Yankees I'm going to finish them!" His good fist flailed at the air. "I don't care what it costs! How could you men have let this happen?"

William decided he better get out of there. Once blame started being passed around, some might end up on him. He knew he had tried to sound the alarm last night, but maybe he didn't do enough. Maybe he would be in huge trouble, and when they found out his Pa was a Yankee soldier, maybe they would hang him as a spy. Right now he just wanted to be back with his Company and away from all this anger.

William tied the courier's horse to a post and slipped away into the frosty morning. He was out of the yard and through the fence gate, blending with the anonymous soldiers milling about the mansion, and he failed to hear General Hood calling him.

"Some private came in here last night to warn us. Find that man! He's the only soldier in this army brave enough to have tried to warn me. When we find him I'm promoting him to sergeant on the spot!"

But William had vanished into the morning mists.

By the time William found the Company they had already gotten the message to move out. The 2nd Tennessee and the rest of General Cleburne's division were heading north to Nashville.

William had an exciting homecoming when Captain Richardson, Louis and the other men saw him. He didn't really have time to explain where he'd been, but everyone was just glad to see him alive.

Lieutenant Jones and his squad had made it back safely, but were upset that they had lost young William. Lieutenant Jones gave him a big grin and clapped his back when he saw him.

First Sergeant Dillard, on the other hand, growled at him.

"Off playin' hookey again, eh boy?" He leaned down in his face. "Did you run off when things got hot last night? I'll be watchin' you Sweeney. You keep yer' nose clean an' do what yer' told." William could feel his face flush like he did back home when his Pa had scolded him for trying to get out of his chores.

William knew he had done his best last night. How could he ever explain to the First Sergeant all he had been through? And would he even agree he had done things right? Did he really wake General Hood, the commander of the whole army, in the middle of the night?! What had he been thinking?!

William took his place in line beside Corporal Heck and the Company moved off down the farm road behind them. They joined a long column as the three divisions of General Cheatham's corps moved through Spring Hill. They passed through the abandoned Federal earthworks surrounding the town, and William saw several dead men lying in heaps in the fields around them. William saw a dead Yankee lying by the road. His shoes and socks and jacket had been stripped off and his bare white feet stood out against the dark red earth. William looked close, expecting every second to see his dead Pa's face staring back at him, but it was someone else's father laying there dead that cold morning. Tears began to stream down his face as he looked at this poor man, alone on this field far from home. Louis put his hand on his shoulder and looked at him knowingly.

They met another stream of soldiers coming into Spring Hill. This was General Stephen Lee's corps and the cannon and wagons of the rest of the army left behind to keep the Federals in their trenches at Columbia. They were just arriving after marching all night. Everyone looked tired and somber.

First Sergeant Dillard detailed one of their slightly wounded men to sit by the road and guide Sergeant Ambers with the wagon when he passed by.

"We're taking the Pike to Franklin. When you see Sergeant Ambers, you bring him up this road until you see one of our boys waiting for you. They'll guide you to us," the First Sergeant said.

Unlike yesterday, Cheatham's corps wasn't leading today. Thousands of men from General Stewart's corps had gone up the Pike before them, which was a real shame. The Federal army that had moved through here the night before had abandoned a large amount of equipment along the road. Entire wagons brimming with supplies had been left in the ditches, pushed off by the retreating men, their teams of mules shot down in their harnesses.

Knapsacks by the hundreds were strewn by the road, their contents spilled and rifled by the passing Confederates ahead of them.

Anything of value had already been taken by the deprived Confederates, but men constantly broke ranks to search through the debris.

William watched desperately for shoes. The Columbia Pike was not the soft red dirt of the farm roads they were used to, but was covered in white gravel, now stained with the blood of shoeless men.

William told the story of the previous night's adventures to Louis. Several other men were within earshot.

"You must have zigged when you should have zagged," Corporal Heck laughed as William described coming out of the woods on the wrong side.

"We're glad you made it back, William," Captain Richardson said again. "Lieutenant Jones was beside himself for losing you. We were sure not looking forward to explaining to Sergeant Ambers that we lost you in the woods."

Louis plied William with a thousand questions.

"I can't believe I wasn't with you," Louis said. "I'd have shot myself a Yank or two."

William thought about his close call with the Federal column and was glad Louis was not there. One shot and the whole line would have fired on them. William was glad he had made it through last night.

He could tell the Company's blood was up. The men knew they had missed a great opportunity to deal the Federals a serious blow, and now they were playing catch up again. Much better to hit them from the back or side. These men knew the Federals at Nashville had had almost three years to prepare their defenses around the city.

In Atlanta the soldiers had learned how difficult it was to carry prepared positions. With good trenches, very few frontal assaults carried the day.

They had been posted on the flanks of Kennesaw Mountain, outside Atlanta, and had watched the Union assaults destroy themselves against the Confederate trenches with great carnage.

"If we move quickly enough," Captain Richardson told them as they marched, "Perhaps we can catch them before they get out of Franklin and before they can get strong breastworks up. The Harpeth River runs north of Franklin, so maybe we can pin them there."

Captain Richardson told them about Franklin as they marched toward the town. He had grown up there and his parents lived there still. He had not seen them for several years, not since the war began. All his kin lived there too, and he raised an eyebrow at William - "Including my cousin Mattie." William blushed.

The Captain talked away the miles to Franklin, and William could see many of the men were getting excited about being so close to the homes they left so long ago. By midday they were just a few miles away, and some of the men began to recognize local people who lined the road to cheer them on. There were many emotional reunions along this road as sons saw parents and wives saw husbands for the first time in years.

Late in the morning a soldier broke ranks and excitedly ran to the head of the column to see Captain Richardson.

"Sir, Sir!" He said excitedly. First Sergeant Dillard scowled at him, but Captain Richardson waved him down.

"How may I help you Private Groom," the Captain said.

"Sir, my house is just up ahead about a quarter mile. I'll tell you sir," he said breathlessly, "I didn't think I'd ever see my Ma and Pa again. Can I run ahead sir and see my dear parents for a few minutes. I'll rejoin the company as soon as you get there, sir."

"Run along Groom," said Captain Richardson. "Be waiting for us when we get there." Groom bounded away, cartridge box, rifle and canteen bouncing as he ran. William watched him run up the column and envied him.

"Good luck Groom!"

"Get us some vittles!"

"I want to meet that sister who writes those sweet letters!" The men of Company A called to Groom's back.

"When we get to Franklin," Captain Richardson called back to the men behind him as they trudged along, "I want you all to meet my mother and father. I want them to meet this fine band of patriots I've served with for these long years. You men do me proud!" The company let out a rebel yell for their beloved captain.

"One more ridge line to get over, and then this road runs right into Franklin," the Captain said, as much to himself as to the men around him. "Up on a little rise at the edge of town lies Mr. Carter's house. One of his sons, Tod Carter, is a captain in General Bates' division. He and I have been friends for many years. It will be exciting to wave to his family as we march by. Three blocks past them and we'll come to the lane my family lives on. My house is the third one on the right." His eyes took on a dreamy quality. "My father is a merchant in town, and brokers farm equipment for this area."

"Will we really get to see your family sir?" William asked.

"I should think so, Private Sweeney. My guess is that the Federals will have cleared out of Franklin and burned the bridges over the Harpeth. We won't see them again until we get to Nashville. We'll be sleeping in Franklin tonight boys!" he shouted to the sky.

Captain Richardson's excitement was contagious, and Company A, 2nd Tennessee Cavalry (dismounted), swung along the road with a spring to their step.

Soon they saw a little clapboard house on the east side of the Pike. The barn behind it had seen better times, and most of the fence rails surrounding the farm were gone, probably burned for firewood by passing troops. There on the front porch was a beaming Private Groom, standing next to a lively old man and a bonneted lady. Several children pranced around their legs.

Private Groom called from the front porch, "Ma and Pa Groom, meet Company A!" Tears rolled down his filthy cheeks, running white streaks from his eyes. His arms wrapped tightly around his parents' shoulders.

Captain Richardson called "Company! Eyes Right!" The men crisply turned their heads while the Captain saluted and the colors dipped for Private Groom and his family. The men cheered and the children danced and Private Groom hugged his parents and his brothers and sisters before running back toward the company and falling back into formation.

William noticed Private Groom had new shoes and a bulging haversack of food. He also noticed that all the following companies cheered the old couple, and even Colonel Granville, the regimental commander, tipped his hat.

It was a spectacular day, warmer than any so far. They had a good road, and the men's spirits soared as they marched north to Franklin.

CHAPTER 15

READY TO FIGHT

Early in the afternoon, the large Confederate column approached the outskirts of Franklin, just 12 miles north of Spring Hill. Couriers rode up and down the line, and William even saw General Cleburne, their division commander, ride by in a new uniform toward the head of the column. The men cheered as he passed.

General Cleburne was very popular with the men. He had fought in every major battle of the Army of Tennessee. His nickname was "Stonewall of the West," after the hard hitting Stonewall Jackson, dead over a year now in Virginia. General Hood considered General Cleburne and his division the best in the army.

As General Cleburne rode by the company, William asked Captain Richardson about Mattie. His mind was not on the march at all, but on the girl who lived in Franklin.

"She's a wonderful young lady, Private Sweeney. She's fourteen, I believe - the same as you. Her father is my father's younger brother, and has been in Virginia fighting with General Lee for three years now. She told me that she now divides her time between her home in Franklin, near ours, and The Athenaeum in Columbia, where she just became a student three months ago. She's grown up a lot since I saw her last," Captain Richardson said. "When I left to join the army, she was just a kid with freckles and pig tails."

The war had changed much about the South. Four years ago, William would not have been in the same class as Mattie, but with men of standing like Captain Richardson mixing with the common men of his company, the Captain had grown to judge men more by their character than their upbringing. He liked William in the short time he had known him, and if he survived the war, the Captain thought, might make a fine man someday.

The column moved up a long straight ascent to a ridge running east to west. "From the top of that ridge you can see Franklin!" the Captain called back to the men. William knew many of the men of Company A were from this small town. They cheered wildly.

They began to hear the notes of a band playing martial tunes just over the rise, and noticed a beehive of activity at the top. Couriers seemed to be riding back and forth, and they began to see Regimental colors moving, not straight down the road, but off to the right.

As they crested the hill they beheld a marvelous sight. Across a mile and a half of open field lay the little town of Franklin - encircled with Federal entrenchments. Captain Richardson's prediction that the Yankees would abandon the town and cross the river proved to be wrong. They seemed determined to make a stand.

William saw the turmoil in his Captain's features. There, less than a twenty minute stroll away, stood his home. A home he had not seen in three years of terrible war. And right in his path lay two lines of Federal troops, watched over by artillery in the line and in the fort north of the river.

The Union lines were imposing. They ringed Franklin in a horseshoe, with the ends facing north and anchored on the bends of the river. Inside the horseshoe lay the town. The breastworks were 4 feet tall in some places and topped by "head logs" so the defenders could shoot under them and be protected from incoming fire. Cannons poked out of embrasures covering the fields in front.

Curiously, about half a mile in front of the fortifications two or three thousand Union troops were spread out on either side of the Columbia Pike in a thin line. They seemed to be trying to dig in, but they were in a very exposed position with the Confederate army spreading out in the fields in front of them.

William followed the Captain as he marched the company past the band that played by the road. William recognized it as the same band that played three nights ago at the mansion - the night he met Mattie.

On the right side of the Pike, the lead corps under General Stewart was spread out across the fields all the way to the river. William watched in awe as thousands of Confederates swarmed across the farmland and formed into splendid ranks. A few cannons set up amongst them, and William watched the couriers and officers ride to and fro as they set the army in place.

He could also see large masses of cavalry moving down toward the river bank way off to the east, and wondered if that was the cavalry of the famous General Forrest.

General Cleburne sat his horse next to the road and directed the officers to the placement of their regiments. Colonel Granville rode up to Captain Richardson and shouted, "Word is that we're going to hit them before dark! We've finally got them cornered with their backs to the river. If we crack their line, we'll destroy their army today. Isn't this your home town, Captain Richardson?"

"Yes, sir," the Captain called back.

"Do your duty today, men and the town will be yours again! There will be no skirmishers today, Captain. Your men will be pure infantry, and I want you right in the line. Form there next to Lowery's men. We're moving in column, so close up nicely. I'll form the rest of the Regiment to your left."

Captain Richardson saluted and led the company off the road and followed the deploying men in front. As they approached their place in line, the sun sank lower in the western sky. Long shadows formed from the men and made everything stand out in stark relief. The Indian summer day still had a little left to it.

"First Sergeant," the Captain Called Dillard. "Form the men 10 across and 6 deep. I want you and Lieutenant Jones at the rear to keep order. I'll keep Corporal Heck and the colors with me at the front. Put the two boys," he motioned to William and Louis, "in the rear with you to help the wounded."

Dillard and Lieutenant Jones formed the ranks when they reached their position in the stubbly field. Two paces to their left another regiment was doing the same thing, and the sight repeated itself for almost a mile down toward the river, and almost that far on the other side of the pike. Six full divisions of gray-clad Confederates, banners flying in the afternoon sun, formed an incredible mass of seething men topped with bayonets.

"Check your ammunition, men, and fix bayonets," First Sergeant Dillard growled. "Take a sip now from your canteens, but make sure they stay full. You'll be wantin' that water a lot more in an hour. Anybody empty?" About a dozen canteens went up. "Collect those canteens, boys," he called to William and Louis, and run back to that well over there and fill 'em. Hurry!"

William and Louis grabbed the canteens and ran back to a well fifty yards behind them at a small farm house. They had to wait for what seemed an eternity to get a turn at the well since there were already a dozen men ahead of them, getting water for their own companies. When they finally made it back, they saw Private Groom passing out pieces of salt pork he carved off a ham he got from home, just an hour ago.

"Enjoy, men," he said as he passed it out. "It's going to be hard work for us today so we might as well have something in our bellies." William passed out the canteens and took a bite of the proffered salt pork. It was heaven! He had been living off walnuts and some pumpkin seeds he had found on the march, and it seemed forever since he had Miss Mattie's sweet cake.

The men rested on their rifles and stood around and talked quietly while they waited. For William, the sight was incredible. Two other divisions had come on to the field and moved into position to the left of their own. Now, this side of the line, heading west from where William stood was also densely packed with Confederate formations.

Lieutenant Jones spoke to the boys. "You'll never see the likes of this again, boys. We've got two full Army Corps, 20,000 men, spread out across these big open fields. I've never seen anything like it. We may be right at the center of the biggest charge of the whole war. Pickett's charge at Gettysburg was only 12,000 or 13,000 men. You are right in the thick of it here."

First Sergeant Dillard said to them, "Keep your focus, boys. It's going to get real terrible, real fast. You're going to see men hit and lose arms and legs and be horribly hurt." He reached into his coat and pulled out a dozen hardwood sticks he'd been whittling for a week on the march and handed half to William and half to Louis.

"Take off your blankets and tear them into strips like this," and he took William's bed roll he carried over his shoulder and tore strips off. "When a man goes down, check to see where he's hit. If it's in the head or the chest or the body, remember where he is and keep on going. If he's hit in an arm or a leg, tie a tourniquet around his limb above the wound and use this stick to wrap it tight. It'll keep him from bleeding to death until the ambulance corps comes along or we can get back to him. Make it tight and run after us."

Both boys began to tear their blankets into strips. "Don't worry about your blankets, neither. They'll be plenty of them lying around after this day's done."

The reality of what was going to happen began to set in on William and Louis and the blood drained from their faces. They went about their tasks, and when they were ready, they looked towards the company again. All the men had little pieces of paper pinned to their backs with their names on them. Off to the left, a group of men gathered around Reverend Campbell, their regimental chaplain, asking him to hold something valuable they might have so it could be sent home if they were killed today. William heard him say that he couldn't hold anything for them today because he was going in with them. All the heads bowed as Reverend Campbell said a short prayer. The men then returned to their places in the ranks, and the chaplain fell in with Colonel Granville's staff as they formed out in front of the regiment.

"Lieutenant Jones," Louis asked and the Lieutenant turned back to him. "Do we need those?" His voice quivered as he pointed to the little tags on the other soldier's coats.

"I'm afraid you do, boys." The Lieutenant answered.

"Neither one of us can write, sir," William said a little sheepishly, "can you do it for us?"

Lieutenant Jones pulled a small pencil from his leather bag and wrote on the two slips of paper:

Pvt Wm Sweeney

2nd Tennessee Cav

and

Pvt Louis Nix

2nd Tennessee Cav

and pinned the slips to the back of their jackets. If they fell in battle, at least they could be identified.

CHAPTER 16
DYING LIKE MEN

It took two hours for the line to form, and it was massive. The officers who had been talking amongst themselves out in front of the lines, raced back and called their men to attention. All along the two mile line, Colonels and Majors and Captains and Lieutenants called "Shoulder Arms," and in a mighty heave, 20,000 rifles moved to the shoulders of the Army of Tennessee. Battle Flags flew from the peaks of hundreds of flag staffs, and officers dashed across the field with swords held high. The regimental bands played "Dixie" and "Bonnie Blue Flag."

"Forward, March!" and they were off. It was awe-inspiring and William stepped off with his company, Captain Richardson in the lead.

Past the moving backs of the men in front, William saw the first puffs of smoke from the cannon in the fortifications. The explosions in the fields to their front seemed tiny compared to their mass. The next time one of the Yankee cannons fired, William happened to be looking right at it, and to his amazement, he could actually see the shell as it flew towards him. The 12 pound solid shot hit about a hundred yards to his right and about a hundred short, but rather than explode, it bounded up like a rock skipped off a pond and flew on into one of the regiments in General French's division, scattering several men like match sticks. For a moment, William was paralyzed by the sight, but then Sergeant Dillard slapped him on the back and he moved forward again.

They moved at a fast walk, trying to cover the ground quickly. William thought again of his father, and tried to block the thought of him waiting in those blue lines across the field.

'A' Company moved parallel to a railroad line that disappeared into the Federal earthworks, and William realized he'd never been on a train. His mind raced to all kind of things he had never done, and he wanted more than anything to live through today so he could do some of them.

More cannon fire now, and he started to hear the small crackle of rifle fire. The Yankee brigades out in front of their line seemed to realize they were in the path of a juggernaut, and as the Confederate moved closer to them, they began to fire rapidly. Most of it was directed at the Federal regiments to his left, William noticed. It looked like his regiment would bypass them, or take them in the flank.

The smoke from the Federal rifles seemed to hang in the air, and soon individuals firing became just red sheets of fire stabbing from the smoke. William could hear some Confederate firing now to his left as the whole line continued to surge forward. It grew more and more intense. William saw some fallen men stagger back from a regiment to the west, and he concentrated on the backs of the men to his front.

The gray line simply overwhelmed the exposed Federals, and William saw them break ranks and turn and run back down the road and toward the breastworks. As soon as they broke, he heard officers call over the din, "Follow them in boys! Follow them in!"

With a maddening Rebel Yell the men began to race forward. 600 yards, now 500. On they ran. The Yankee soldiers in the entrenchments didn't want to fire into their own troops, so they held their fire until most of them had entered their lines. 300 yards, 200. Even with some Federal soldiers still outside their lines, the Yankees could wait no more.

Thousands of Yankee rifles fired at once, and a living sheet of flame and smoke and deadly missiles poured into the advancing Confederates. William thought he had stepped into a hornet's nest as the air came alive with moving sheets of lead. William sensed, rather that actually saw, entire ranks of Rebel soldiers absorb this impact and fall screaming.

The company kept running forward, but in seconds, half a dozen men had fallen. The company just put their heads down and moved right over them.

Lieutenant Jones was waving his sword and First Sergeant Dillard grabbed William's collar and pointed to the wounded men, and then he was gone, following the company. William moved like a machine, horrified at the grotesque sights he saw.

The first man he came to was sitting on the ground, holding his stomach and moaning. Remembering what the Sergeant had told him, he stopped long enough to confirm that it was private Wallace, and then moved on to the next man. This time he wrapped a tourniquet around a shattered arm and was soaked with blood in seconds. He could not look into the man's eyes. He saw Louis bend over a man, and empty his stomach on the ground before moving on.

They did what they could and were off to find the Company in the smoke and confusion. Volley after volley poured from the Federal lines into the advancing Confederates. The roar of cannon punctuated the continuous rattle of rifle fire. Every step William took put him practically on top of a dead or wounded man. Within 100 yards he had used up all his tourniquets and seemed to be just stumbling blindly behind the company into the inferno. He couldn't see Louis and he prayed his friend was alright.

A huge Rebel Yell caused him to look up from a wounded soldier and he saw the company's battle flag just 20 yards away above the smoke, and realized Corporal Heck had made it to the top of the breastwork. He sprinted to the colors, glad to know that someone had survived this massacre and wanting to be close to someone he knew.

He pulled his rifle off his back, and checked the percussion cap. The roar was deafening and his eyes stung from the acrid smoke, but he kept moving forward. A gust of wind seemed to blow the smoke away for one brief moment and he saw the Yankee breastworks had been captured and A Company and a lot more Confederates were in the works!

William was still behind the four foot wall and realized most of the shots were going over his head. He tended two wounded men, sitting at the base of the wall, but there was little he could do for them. He looked to his left and right for Louis, but could not find him in the mass of men still clambering over the breastworks or hobbling back from it. There was too much smoke to see very far in any direction.

William lay for a few seconds and caught his breath against the embankment. He could hear a terrific battle on the other side. He took a deep breath, heaved himself over the top, and froze as he saw the carnage below. Dead and dying men covered every inch of ground, and William could see a seething mass of men fighting desperately up beside a large building.

There was nothing else he could do for the wounded now. He really wasn't sure if anyone from A Company was still fighting. He couldn't see anyone clearly, and the air was absolutely alive with flying bullets. They tugged at his clothes and he felt one's hot breath whiz by his cheek.

William realized he was crouched at the top of the embankment for all to see, so he plunged down into the cauldron and moved to try to find the company. Finally, he saw the company battle flag over the smoke and moved toward it. Another Confederate regiment poured over the breastwork and William was carried right up to the back of a small building where he stumbled into the back of another soldier. The man turned around and William was looking into the face of Lieutenant Jones who stared wild-eyed at him for a second and then turned and raised his sword again.

William was suspended between masses of moving, writhing men. To his horror he realized he was standing on a dead Federal soldier.

The firing all around him was continuous and deadly. For a moment, the mass of men moved forward and William found himself at the front of the firing line. Men were aiming toward the smoke to his front and he saw the Union Flag waving just a few paces away. He cocked and fired his rifle again and again before he realized he had to reload it. They were firing at him from over there, and he fumbled for a cartridge and rammed it home and started firing back.

William soon realized he was standing shoulder to shoulder with Corporal Heck holding the colors. A group of Federal soldiers broke from their mass and ran toward them. William fired and felt the explosion of a rifle right over his shoulder as someone else fired from behind him. When the smoke cleared briefly, he saw that the group of Yankees were all down.

Captain Richardson appeared from nowhere and waved them forward. The mass of Confederates surged ahead right up into some family's yard. William fought hand to hand with a Union soldier for a split second, and then a volley from more Federals killed his antagonist and several Rebels around him. William watched in terror as Captain Richardson was struck. He spun, crumpled to the ground, and did not rise.

That volley took some of the fight out of the Confederate line and William followed Corporal Heck in a mad dash back toward the embankment. They scrambled up and William saw dozens of puffs of dirt in the fading light as the Federals fired again and again after them.

The few remaining men of Company A scrambled to the other side of the embankment and fired back into the cauldron. Those down in the ditch reloaded rifles for the shooters at the top.

Corporal Heck planted the colors in the dirt at the top of the wall and, taking the rifle from a dead man's hand, fired at the advancing Federals. William handed his rifle to the Corporal and reloaded the dropped one. Other men were doing the same all around him. Men scrambled around for more ammunition from the dead and dying.

William had no time to realize darkness had fallen. His entire world was reduced to a few yards of horror as he loaded and loaded. Soon, Corporal Heck slid down the embankment, a bloody gash in his forehead, and another gray-jacket took his place. Before long, he was shot down too.

Lieutenant Jones, lying next to William, peered through a gap in the head log and yelled, "Here they come!"

Dozens of Confederates leapt to the top and fired a tremendous volley at the advancing Federals, but they could not stop the onslaught. Many of the men on the crest were shot down, and others tried to take their place, but the fire was too great.

"They're right on the other side of the bank," Lieutenant Jones yelled. "Don't let 'em over the top!"

The Federal line lay on one side of the five-foot embankment and the Confederates lay on the other side. The men would raise their rifles over their heads and try to fire down into each other. In the twilight, Confederates searched for rifles with bayonets, and they would hurl them like spears over the embankment to impale the enemy on the other side. Finally, as darkness fell heavily on the tortured earth, the fighting began to die down.

William lay on the bodies in the ditch and tried to get Corporal Heck's wound to stop bleeding. Heck was in a lot of pain, but it did not look mortal. He could look up and still see the flag flying above his head.

Finally, after what seemed like hours, William heard the Federals pulling out. There was nothing the few exhausted survivors of A Company could do except lay there and hope they were gone for good. Lieutenant Jones moved among the men and tried to sort out who was left.

"There's twelve of us left here," he told William, "and First Sergeant Dillard's got about ten more on the other side of these Alabama boys." The units were all mixed up. "That gives us twenty-two out of sixty-two that left this morning. We'll find a few more, we hope."

When Lieutenant Jones said he didn't think the Federals were over there at all anymore, William crawled over the embankment with the young officer to find the Captain. They searched for half an hour through the wreckage of the battlefield before William found him alive but unconscious.

CHAPTER 17

CARNAGE

Captain Richardson was soaked in blood. He was surrounded by dead and dying men, and Lieutenant Jones had to help William lift a dead soldier off his legs to get to him. The night was dark and they couldn't tell which side the dead man had sacrificed his life for, blue or gray. The moaning and crying from all the shattered men was heart wrenching.

William held the Captain's unconscious head in his lap while Lieutenant Jones crawled back to the embankment to gather the rest of the exhausted company. William wept for his wounded Captain, for Louis, whom he had not seen since the charge, and for all the men that lay dead around him.

"You'll be okay, Captain," William said through his tears. "We'll get you home and they'll take care of you." He said this over and over as he held the Captain. William felt around Captain Richardson's arms and chest, trying to find the wound, and finally identified a blood soaked spot in his right shoulder. He also found that his hand supporting the Captain's head and shoulders was also soaked in blood. Perhaps a bullet had gone through his body without striking anything vital. William prayed with all his might for that to be the case.

Many men were searching for friends across the bloody ground. Some lanterns had finally arrived and, as far as William could see in the darkness, there was a field of men on the ground and small groups looking for the wounded by lamp light. Some were obviously from the town, because he saw lights descending the hill from that direction.

"Sweeney? Private Sweeney?!" he heard Lieutenant Jones' tired voice call.

"Here, sir," William answered, and Lieutenant Jones came to him through the darkness. He had his men with him, and William could make them out stopping and checking the wounded in the darkness. Corporal Heck, with a bloody bandage wrapped around his head, still carried the company guidon and limped next to Lieutenant Jones.

"Company A, 2nd Tennessee!" Lieutenant Jones stood erect and called loudly several times to the darkness. "If you're wounded out there, call to us! We'll find you. The guidon is here with Corporal Heck. Come to us if you can. We're looking for you boys! We'll find you!" Lieutenant Jones sent one man up the road to the top of the little hill. "Keep watch for us in case they come back. If you see civilians from town, tell them to come help." William watched this man move toward the north and disappear.

"Corporal Heck," William said to the wounded color-bearer. "Have you seen Louis Nix?" Heck shook his head.

"I'm sorry, William, I haven't seen him since the charge. First Sergeant Dillard and his survivors are looking for wounded along the side of the wall," referring to the embankment so many men had died on, "and they're sure to find him. He is not with our group. That I know. Let me see the Captain."

William held the battle flag aloft for the men to guide on and every minute or so he shouted "2nd Tennessee!"

"The Captain's wounded in the right shoulder, front and back," William said,

Corporal Heck expertly searched the Captain for other wounds and came back to the shoulder. He took a blanket from a dead man nearby and tore off strips. He wadded two balls of cloth, placed them over the two wounds, and wound the long strips round and round the Captain with William's help.

"This'll stop the bleeding, I hope," Heck said. "If we can keep him from bleeding to death right here, perhaps he's got a fightin' chance."

William was concentrating hard on bandaging the Captain, but he kept up his chant. When they had him wrapped and laid back on the ground, he noticed macabre figures groping their way to him in the darkness. Private Groom was one of the first he saw. His ashen face peered out of the darkness and nearly scared William to death.

Corporal Heck noticed Groom and helped him to the ground beside the Captain. William and Corporal Heck checked him over and found him shot and bleeding all over, one ear gone, missing two fingers, two holes in an arm, one in and one out. His face had terrible cuts, as if some giant's club had sliced its way across him from hairline to chin. Groom could not speak.

By the time Lieutenant Jones came back from searching for men, a dozen wounded men had crawled or limped over to William and Corporal Heck. Louis was not among them and William's heart sank. The Indian summer day was rapidly turning into a cold night.

"We've got to get these men to shelter," Lieutenant Jones said. "I've been over to First Sergeant Dillard and he's collecting men over there," he motioned south over the embankment.

"Let's load all we can carry and try to get to Captain Richardson's house. It's just a short walk and we can get inside there. Corporal Heck, you stay here with the guidon until First Sergeant Dillard comes up and I'll be back to get you and guide the others.

Other companies were doing the same thing all around them. There seemed to be no officers except lieutenants around, and also no stretcher parties from the ambulance corps. William sensed from the way the other men acted that this battle had been a catastrophe, and the poorly equipped Confederate support units were just overwhelmed.

William and Lieutenant Jones hoisted the Captain between them and struggled under his dead weight. The other men all had hold of a wounded comrade and their little band stumbled toward town. Several of the wounded had to stay behind with Corporal Heck and wait for the next trip.

Some townspeople met them before they had gone very far. They wanted to help, so Lieutenant Jones and his small band quickly found willing assistants. These people knew the Richardson family, and a wagon and mule were quickly produced and took the trio on to the house. William rode with the Captain's head cradled in his lap and looked around at the devastation.

The moon was out now, and all around him he saw limping, struggling men. They all seemed to be wandering aimlessly trying to find shelter or help. The groans and screams of the wounded could be heard everywhere. Lights blazed in most of the houses and the people of Franklin opened their homes to the injured of both armies.

Lieutenant Jones' little band turned down a side street and stopped in front of a tidy two-story clapboard house with a wide front porch. Lights blazed, and a few wounded men were already there. William and Lieutenant Jones lifted Captain Richardson off the wagon, and leading the way, carried him up the front steps of his house.

"Mrs. Richardson! Mrs. Richardson!" Lieutenant Jones called out to the house as they came to the front door. "It's Samuel Jones, and I have John with me. He's hurt bad!" Mrs. Richardson appeared at the door, her face twisted with worry.

"Get him in the back room quickly," she said as she took charge of the care of her son. "Mattie," she called to her niece.

As William and Lieutenant Jones laid the Captain on the bed in the back bedroom, Mattie rushed in carrying more bandages. She briefly looked at William, and then she and Mrs. Richardson went to work.

CHAPTER 18

THE WOUNDED

William made three trips with the wagon that night back to the horrors of the battlefield. Lieutenant Jones and the survivors of A Company searched through the bodies for their comrades, and took all they found back to the Richardson house, where Mattie and Mrs. Richardson bandaged and cared for them.

William was the only one searching for Yankee dead and wounded. Lieutenant Jones stopped him as he gently raised the head of a Union soldier laying face down beside the road.

"William, how come you're searching through these damned Yankees?" he said harshly.

The tears burst from William's eyes. "My father's a Union soldier, sir. They took him a year ago and we don't know where he is!" William's dark secret was out, and he didn't care who knew. He was terrified that his poor father might lie among these Union dead.

Lieutenant Jones' face softened. "I'm sorry, William." He put his arm around the sobbing boy's shoulders. "If you find him son, we'll take care of him. It's a bad night for us all."

William searched until he almost dropped from exhaustion. He called his father's name over and over but he got no reply. Finally, he staggered back to the Richardson house.

Before long, First Sergeant Dillard arrived with Sergeant Ambers and Henry and the wagon loaded with A Company men. Louis, in tatters but very much alive, was there too, leaning on Sergeant Amber's shoulder.

William leapt up on the seat and embraced his friends. None of them could speak about the terrible night, and the two wagons rumbled with their organized load of dead and dying men down the road and into the Richardson's yard, where they all collapsed for the night.

When daylight came, the survivors took stock. A Company had started the previous morning with 62 men and officers. Lieutenant Jones and First Sergeant Dillard were both alive and relatively unscathed. Now only nineteen soldiers, including William, Sergeant Ambers and Louis, were all that remained of the Company. They didn't count Henry on the rolls but he worked hard to help the wounded.

Captain Richardson and eighteen other men were found wounded and convalesced at the Richardson's home. Some of them would not make it through the day or week. Twelve bodies of A Company men were found on the battlefield and the rest were just gone. Whether they had been captured, or just drifted away, they would never know.

The whole Confederate Army of Tennessee was in similar straights. Almost two thousand men and officers had been killed, and nearly five thousand more were either wounded, captured or missing. General Cleburne was dead, as was Colonel Granville. Five general officers had already been found dead, several more were seriously wounded, and one was a prisoner. Many other units were just as shattered as A Company.

First Sergeant Dillard woke the exhausted men at daybreak. The survivors huddled around the wagon under the scraps of blankets they had. Most had torn theirs up for bandages. Some local boys of 9 or 10 had come out of surrounding houses and started a fire for the men, and they stood gawking at the Confederate soldiers as they pulled themselves together. Somewhere, coffee was produced, and the men filled their cups with the steaming beverage they had not tasted in many months.

The sounds from the Richardson house were quieter now, as the wounded lay exhausted everywhere. The men from A Company wandered through the house speaking quietly with their less fortunate comrades and providing words of encouragement. First Sergeant Dillard organized a detail to bury several men who had not lived through the night.

"William, go fetch Louis. Let's get a letter posted back home to let our kin know the situation. There will be some sad folks in Fayettetown," Sergeant Ambers said quietly, "and our people need to know we survived.

Sergeant Ambers composed the letter and wrote it out with his left hand.

> December 1, 1864
> Dear Family and Friends in Fayettetown,
> We have fought a desperate battle at Franklin and have come through alive. We are posting this with Mrs. Richardson of Franklin, mother of our Captain who is seriously wounded. Louis Nix, William Sweeney, and John Ambers of A Company 2nd Tennessee Cavalry, have all survived unwounded. We have no word yet of the other Fayettetown men, as we are all split up. Send some one to Mrs. Richardson soon because there is a strong chance some are hurt.
> Pray for us.
> Your Obedient Servant,
> John Ambers

William took the note to the house. He stepped lightly past the men on the porch and in the parlor, and walked to the back room where Captain Richardson lay.

Mattie sat in a chair next to his bed, holding his pale hand, her eyes closed. Her apron was stained with the blood of wounded men, but she looked beautiful to William, even through her exhaustion.

She opened her eyes at William's approach and a glimmer of recognition flashed through them.

"Thank you for bringing John home to us," she said softly. You're the young man who guarded our carriage, are you not?" Her voice sounded weary, but strong.

"I am Miss. My name is William Sweeney. I'm one of your cousin's runners." William was too tired for much formality. "How is he?"

"He's hurt badly, but at least he's here in our care, and we'll do all that can be done. It appears that a bullet passed cleanly through his shoulder. We don't know yet if permanent damage is done." As she said this, her eyes stayed fixed on William.

"Your cousin is a fine man and a beloved officer, ma'am," William said. "We are all with him in his time of need." He handed her the letter. "Our folks in Fayettetown will hear of this terrible battle and will worry about us mightily. Can you see this is posted to them? I can't find Mrs. Richardson. I'd be much obliged, Miss. We have also asked that they send help to your home to find the rest of the men from our county who might need help. When we're gone, will you watch for men from Lincoln County?

She took the paper and nodded soberly. "I will do that for you..." she looked at him questioningly.

"William, Miss," he said. "William Sweeney."

"And I am Mattie Richardson, cousin to your Captain. I am sure he would've introduced us properly if only ..." her gaze shifted toward the Captain and tears welled up in her eyes.

"Yes, ma'am, I'm sure he would. We spoke of you on the march here. He is very proud of you."

William heard a commotion outside. "I must go, Miss." He gestured to the Captain, "Tell him our prayers are with him. The Lord will help you watch over him."

Mattie smiled tiredly and watched as William turned and left.

CHAPTER 19
REGROUP

General Hood had no choice. Almost a quarter of his army lay wounded or dead at Franklin, but while he grew weaker, the Federals at Nashville grew stronger by the hour. Word had already reached him that another Federal Army Corps with thousands of men was arriving by boat from Missouri, and fresh troops could turn the tide against him. His army had driven the Federals from Franklin, at a terrible cost, but he must move on to Nashville immediately.

Word filtered down to Major O'Rourke, who had assumed command of the 2nd Tennessee with the death last night of Colonel Granville. He found Lieutenant Jones by midmorning.

"Lieutenant Jones, assemble your men in an hour. We're moving out with General Cheatham's corps as soon as we can assemble. Scour the dead back there for their shoes, blankets, and cartridges, as we have another big fight coming. Let's get these men out of this slaughter house as fast as possible before they dwell on our losses too much," Major O'Rourke said.

William went back to the battlefield with Sergeant Ambers and the wagon and a detail of men. The ambulance corps had finally started getting many of the wounded away, but there were still piles of dead men all over the field, and burial details were digging long trenches, wide enough for two men to lie, side by side.

Since most of the dead were Confederates, there was not much to re-supply from. They managed some blankets, ammunition, and several haversacks filled with walnuts and hard tack, but that was about it. It was almost too painful to see the horror of that field by day, and they went demoralized back to the Richardson house. Worst of all, many of the men still had no shoes. William's feet, like those of many other men, still left bloody footprints where they walked. When they returned he re-wrapped his feet in the rags of his old blanket, and it made him think of General Washington's men at Valley Forge in the American Revolution.

The little band of men formed up with Lieutenant Jones and First Sergeant Dillard in the road in front of the Richardson's house. The ladies watched them go from their front porch, and there were many tears among the men as they left wounded comrades of many months behind.

The gravity of their situation was apparent to all when Major O'Rourke formed up the regiment. Sixty five men filled the 2nd Tennessee where almost 200 formed for the attack yesterday afternoon. The losses were devastating. The men, however, shouldered their arms, and, followed by the two remaining company wagons, set off north for Nashville.

William walked with Louis and Sergeant Ambers at the rear of the Company with the wagon. Their poor mules could hardly pull, they were so worn out. The wagon was mostly empty anyway, so that helped. They left Henry back at the Richardson's to help with the wounded. As they crossed the repaired bridge over the Harpeth River toward Nashville, a cold wind began to blow hard into their faces.

CHAPTER 20

DIGGING IN

Nashville lay about eighteen miles north of Franklin in a bend of the Cumberland River. It sat much like the town of Franklin, with the river to its east, north, and west, except on a more massive scale. In 1864, it was one of the most heavily fortified cities in North America.

The Union Army had occupied Nashville early in the war, and had two and a half years to prepare its defenses. It was well supplied from the north by road and rail and from the rivers by steamboat from as far away as St. Louis. Union forces in December 1864 had been concentrating at Nashville for two months when Hood's rag-tag army began its march back into Tennessee.

With the fighting at Franklin, General Hood's army had been greatly reduced, while the Federal's had combined the army of Schofield, who fought at Franklin, with the masses of troops under Union General Thomas at Nashville. Almost 60,000 Union troops were amassed in a huge fortification, facing a little over 20,000 starving, battered Confederates. Hood had sent the rest of his army - General Bate's division and Forrest's cavalry - to Murfreesboro.

Many men of the Army of Tennessee called Nashville home. Like the men from Franklin, they arrived on December 2nd on the outskirts of their homes and looked in disbelief at the Federal works denying them entry to the city they loved. Their mothers and fathers, wives and children were living behind those Federal guns.

The march to Nashville was particularly hard. The Indian summer days of the last week had been replaced by cruel winter weather. The wind howled from the north around the men and froze fingers to rifles and took all feeling from feet, ears, and noses.

William and his comrades were ill prepared for this new onslaught. The closest source for blankets and equipment to the keep the Rebel Army warm – Franklin - was itself inundated with thousands of wounded men that must be cared for.

As the Army of Tennessee moved into position facing the Federal Army at Nashville, their saving grace was the extensive forests that covered the area. General Hood set his Army in a huge semi-circle around the city to its south. For seven miles, the Confederates began constructing fortification of their own to prepare for the Union assault they knew would come. They were too weak to attack the Federal lines, so their only hope was that they could deal a crushing blow to the Yankees as they poured out of their works to attack.

Major O'Rourke's little regiment was placed at the far right of the Confederate line next to a railroad that ran toward Murfreesboro, and then on to Tullahoma, not far from Fayetteville, William's home. Major O'Rourke's small regiment had to cover 300 yards of the line, with no one to back them up.

That meant Lieutenant Jones' depleted A Company had a hundred yards of rolling, wooded terrain to defend with 20 men. They set about it as hard as they could.

Lieutenant Jones called Corporal Heck, First Sergeant Dillard, Sergeant Ambers, and two other A company Sergeants to his little shelter on December 3rd. They had arrived that morning and started cutting trees for shelter and digging entrenchments. The weather was very cold and a large fire roared beside them. William and Louis were both there as the company messengers.

"We're going to build five small, 4-man redoubts in these woods. We'll cut trees and face their branches, all tangled together, in between these positions. We've got to cut as many trees as we can out front to give us clear fields of fire, and we'll use those logs to strengthen our positions and to burn. We've only got two axes, so I want men swinging them 24 hours a day in shifts."

"Sergeant Ambers, you take the boys and scour these farms behind us for any food you can find. Get us a couple of decent meals a day and keep us going. We'll tie in with the regiments on either side of us and we'll be ready when they come. First Sergeant Dillard will give you the details," Lieutenant Jones said. He looked at the men for questions.

These soldiers were professionals, and had built lines like this for months now. They knew from experience that determined men could hold out against almost impossible odds if their defenses were strong.

Every day, William went with Sergeant Ambers to scour the countryside with their tired, old mules. About all they could find was pumpkins. They did have several walnut trees in the slowly disappearing woods around them, and they supplemented their meager rations with those two staples.

One day, they happened upon a group of Confederate soldiers making shoes. They would take a man's old, broken down shoe and wrap animal skin, usually cowhide, hair-side in, around the crumbling shell of the shoe. As the hide dried in the cold, chill air, it would make a wearable moccasin for the soldier. They were making them as fast as they could to meet the demand of the army.

After a few days, the company had built a substantial fortification. They had cleared hundreds of trees to their front and their fighting positions were strong. They had constructed abatis of sharpened stakes all across the front of their line, and dug trenches connecting their redoubts protected by the interlaced tree branches between them.

They kept strong fires going to keep themselves warm, and they were somehow surviving the bitter winter weather. Several of the men came down with terrible eye irritations from the smoke of the fires as they huddled around them for warmth. These men were practically blinded, so they were divided up and tasked to load rifles for the men that could see.

By December 8th, however, they were starving to death. Lieutenant Jones called Sergeant Ambers over. "What's our ration look like today, Sergeant?" he asked the one-armed veteran.

"We can't hardly find anything back there, sir. The countryside is plum cleaned out. And I can't find forage for the mules, either. They're about played out, too," Sergeant Ambers reported glumly.

"That's what I was afraid of, Sergeant" Lieutenant Jones said sadly. "We're going to have to take one of the mules for food. Put the weakest one down, and let's butcher it and see how long she'll last us."

Sergeant Ambers was devastated. He had looked after those old mules like they were his children, and they had carried him all the way from Alabama to here, and he hated to put one down.

He shuffled back over to the boys, and told them the news.

"You know, Sergeant," William replied, "We can make shoes out of her, too. I know you're awfully attached to them, but I'm starving to death and my feet are falling off my legs they're so cold. I'll do it for you."

Sergeant Ambers looked at the mules dejectedly, and walked over and rubbed their muzzles. Then he unhooked the one called "Old Abe" and brought it over to William. He handed him his big navy colt. "Make it clean, boy. Don't let her suffer."

William had killed and butchered animals his whole life and he led "Old Abe" over behind the wagon, and with one shot, put her down. He and Louis butchered her and divided her amongst the men that night, and they feasted.

William skinned her and he and Louis spent the next day making shoes for the men in the company. William had never worked so hard in his life. He knew his father would be surprised at his efforts, and when he finally made a pair for himself, he was proud of his work and finally had warm feet to show for it.

CHAPTER 21

A LETTER

It was certainly disheartening to the men to see the Federal preparations compared to their own. A flotilla of over fifty steamboats had been continuously disembarking Federal soldiers from Missouri. These additional troops meant they were drastically outnumbered and every soldier in A Company knew it. Huge batteries of cannons were constantly being lined up against them while their company had no artillery support.

By December 9th, things had gotten worse. Winter weather had become a more formidable enemy than the Yankees. For four days, freezing rain and 60mph winds howled and froze the men. They were all sick and hacking coughs racked everybody. They had no shelter against the rain and everything was soaked and frozen. Ice a half inch thick formed over everything. It was desperately hard to keep their fires going, and neither man nor beast could keep their footing on the ice that covered the roads and the countryside.

A ray of good cheer arrived on the 14th. The weather warmed a little and a letter arrived addressed to William! Mattie Richardson had sent it several days before by one of the wounded men from

Franklin who had come to rejoin his unit. William asked Sergeant Ambers read it to him.

> Dear Private Sweeney,
> I am sure you will let all of my cousins' soldiers know that the Captain is recovering. He has been up from his sick bed and his wounds seem to be healing well. He sends his regards to you all. He says he will send Lieutenant Jones a note soon.
> I regret to inform you that Private Groom passed to his Maker yesterday. We know this will be a blow to the men, but his Mother had come, and was by his side to ease his passing.
> Take care, William. I hope to see you again.
> Your obd't servant,
> Mattie Richardson

William savored the sound of those last lines for a moment, and then took it straight away to Lieutenant Jones, who read it and looked at him with raised eyebrows.

"Good news for the Captain, bad news for Groom, but good news for you, eh, Sweeney?" A mischievous grin played across his face as he watched William's embarrassment. He handed the letter back to William. "Go tell the men. They'll want the news."

William took a great deal of good natured ribbing from the men over "his sweetheart." When he returned, he sat next to Louis by the fire.

"Louis? Do you think she likes me?" William asked his friend.

"She don't know you like I know you," Louis chided him. Then he relented, "We've grown up a lot in the last couple of months, William. This war won't last forever, and if'n we survive it, we're gonna have a lot of catchin' up to do. Courtin' a girl like that's gonna take some doin', but you've proved to the Cap'n you're as good a man at 14 as many men are a lot older."

"Thanks, Louis," William said. "I think about her all the time," he gestured around him, "even in all of this. I think about Pa, maybe right over there in the Yankee line, or dead. I think about Ma, and Jim and Becky back on the farm and wonder how they are. I feel like I've got such big worries on my mind. It's nice to have pleasant thoughts of Mattie, no matter what happens. I think it's what's getting me through all this."

William sat quietly, and then heaved out a long breath. "I will find a way to see her again."

"That's the spirit, William," Louis clapped him on the shoulder.

The boys rolled up in their soggy blankets and tried to sleep. The warmer air had begun to melt the ice and it dripped from the branches of the lean-to above their heads. A dense fog formed over the ground as they finally slept.

CHAPTER 22
YANKEE ATTACK

Daylight brought back the war. Both boys, with the entire Confederate Army of Tennessee, were awakened by the booming of cannons and the onslaught of the Federal army by the tens of thousands.

"To Arms! To Arms!" Lieutenant Jones came rushing past. "Sweeney! Nix!" he called, "get to the far redoubts and make sure the men are ready. Victory or death is the watchword today!"

The boys were off in flash, rifles banging against their backs. Sergeant Ambers fumbled with his pistol and tried to shake the sleep from his head.

When William arrived at the far post, First Sergeant Dillard was already there, standing with the men peering out into the fog. Most of the noise of battle seemed to be coming from off to the west. William could see the end of the Regiment to their left in position also.

The first charge by the Federals was like a bolt from Hell. A huge mass of blue-coated men appeared out of the fog and began firing on their entire line. As the Confederates returned the fire, it sounded like pop guns against thunder.

Bullets poured over them, and William took a place in the breastwork. He heard the splat of lead bullets battering the log above his head. He fired, reloaded, and fired as fast as he could. He saw some blue soldiers fall and soon the rifle smoke mixed with the lifting fog to obscure everything except the continuous muzzle flashes.

This firing continued for long minutes, but the Federals advanced no further. It seemed there was just enough fire from the Rebel positions to hold them at bay.

The sun began to rise a little higher in the sky and from the small rise A Company occupied in the Confederate line, William could see thousands of Federal infantry advancing on them like a huge, unstoppable wave. So far, none of the men in his redoubt had been hit, but the entire area was alive with flying lead, clipping and spattering amongst the fallen timber.

Within half an hour, William noticed men in gray retreating from way off to his right. They drifted singly, and in twos and threes, through tree stumps behind them heading toward safety. The Federals to William's front kept up there steady fire but did not advance.

Lieutenant Jones came panting into their redoubt. "The regiment to our right is collapsing! We're to fall back toward the Franklin Pike and make a stand! "First Sergeant!" He shouted to Dillard, "This position holds until I can get the rest emptied out and spread out to behind you. When I'm set, you bring your boys!" Dillard nodded and Lieutenant Jones sprinted back the way he came, crouching low as bullets and shells whipped the air above him.

William heard all this and wondered aloud, "There's only five men in this position! We've got to hold all those hundreds and hundreds of men?!" No one heard him as the volleys kept flying.

Minutes later, William saw the rest of the company go running past them to the rear. He saw Louis and Sergeant Ambers with them and thanked God they were safe. He also saw several men fall and not get up. He focused on firing and reloading, firing and reloading. Steam rose from his barrel as it began to glow red hot.

First Sergeant Dillard kept them there for the longest five minutes William ever knew. They could see the Yankees maneuvering around their right, and just when he though it was too late, Dillard yelled "Go!"

The men bolted out of the position. William turned to run and a ball hit the stock of his rifle just as he cleared the edge of the redoubt. It spun him around and knocked him down, and he felt a terrible pain in his hand.

A big meaty fist reached down and grabbed him by the collar and pulled him to his feet. First Sergeant Dillard had seen him fall and had come back for him. Dillard shoved him in the right direction and yelled "Go Sweeney! Git' back to your sweetheart! I'm done runnin'!"

As William ran, he saw the big man stand his ground against the advancing Federals, swing his rifle to his shoulder, and fire. Then, in one easy, practiced motion, he reversed the musket and smashed the stock into the head of the first Yankee to reach him. The next instant, the old veteran was overwhelmed by a wave of blue, and First Sergeant Dillard was no more.

William ran as fast as he could, tears streaming down his face and bullets zipping the air around him. He jumped down into a small sheltered gulley and found it full of Confederate infantry, lying on their stomachs, waiting for the advancing Federals columns.

As William dropped down, a Sergeant pulled his ear close, "Keep on moving private. Your regiment's back there, forming up. We're Texans, and we mean to stop them here. Ya'll got to go help out somewheres else! Hurry!"

He shoved William to his feet and William saw Major O'Rourke forming up the regiment to move. He ran and fell into formation with Corporal Heck, right beside the colors.

"First Sergeant Dillard is dead," he cried, and men turned their heads to hear the news. Then William got a grip on himself, and added, "He saved my life and stood alone against the whole Yankee Army."

Several men nodded in appreciation, and then they were off on the double-quick. They were joined by other Regiments, and William saw a mounted General to their front.

"That's General Smith," Corporal Heck said to him as they ran. "He took General Cleburne's place. Lieutenant Jones says they're moving our division to the whole other side of the line. They got hit real hard over there."

The column ran through a small untended orchard and then crossed a railroad line. They headed out into the open toward the Franklin Pike with the sun at their back, heading west. William saw to his amazement they were running right behind the whole Confederate line, from one end to the other, east to west. He could see two huge Federal columns boiling out of the Nashville defenses in readiness for a new assault on the Confederate fortifications.

Past the Pike now, across a muddy creek that soaked them all to their knees in the frigid water, and then up a small rise. As they crested the hill, another horrible sight greeted them.

Two whole Federal corps, complete with cavalry and artillery, were rolling right over the Confederate line on the left. From the hill, the men could see it like a painting before them. They looked right down through the desultory smoke and fog and could make out wave after wave of blue coated soldiers lapping around the small Rebel forts, and then swallowing them whole.

Off the hill they went, then down into another creek bed. They'd run over two miles by now, cross country, exhausted, carrying their rifles, knowing they were running toward certain death.

They knew they were too small in number to stop a force so huge. They crossed another road. William heard someone call it the Granny White Pike, and William's racing, crazed mind wondered who Granny White was?

They stopped just on the other side of this road and began to form a defensive line at the crest of the hill. William saw there was still a thin line of Confederates between them and the rolling blue juggernaut, so he knew they had a few moments to prepare themselves. He looked around frantically for Louis and Sergeant Ambers. He spotted them and ran to their side. They were panting badly and the entire column of men looked worn out. They seemed to reel about the hill as they dug at the frozen earth with their bare hands to build some protection from the coming onslaught.

"William," Sergeant Ambers gasped, "dig, boy, dig!" Find some logs or something we can get cover behind!" The hill was barren. He took off his bayonet like the other men, and used it to pry stones from the ground. Louis was doing the same thing. For an hour, they clawed the ground like madmen. The whole time, they watched the men in blue move toward the line to their front, and finally, they seemed to merge with the enveloping cloud of smoke.

"Cavalry to the left!" came the shout down the line! Thousands of mounted Union horsemen could be seen in the valley below sweeping majestically around their flank. They were two miles away when they were spotted, but on horseback that would not take long to cover.

Sergeant Ambers called the boys to him. "William, Louis, this looks to be the end. There's no way we can stand here long. That cavalry is going to get behind us unless a miracle happens, and I think General Hood is fresh out of miracles."

He pointed to the rear. "Across this road, it gets really wooded again. Over that way is Franklin Pike. When it gets bad, that's where we're headed. We'll get down in them trees and hope the Yankee cavalry won't follow us in there."

He looked sternly at the boys. "You listen to me, and stick together. If we get split up, we'll meet at Captain Richardson's house in Franklin, and rest up there. It's fifteen miles or more, but we can get there by tomorrow morning. From there, by night, we can make it home in a week if we're careful."

William looked at Sergeant Ambers with astonishment. "You mean we're going to run?" he said. William began to understand that if he made it home alive at all, it wasn't going to be as any hero. He would be staggering home with his tail between his legs, a survivor of a defeated army.

"Darn right, we're running, boy, and you do like I say. We've lost. Look out there," he gestured to the collapsing Rebel army. "By nightfall, this will be a disaster, every man for himself. You've got to live to get back home. It ain't nothin' but survival now!"

The Federal advance was less than a thousand yards away. Lieutenant Jones strode up and down the line. Retreating Confederates began to stream up the hill and through the lines, many stopped, bolstered by courage, or just exhaustion, and joined their defense. William noticed these men either came through the lines looking terrified and wild eyed, or they carried a grim look of acceptance on their faces.

It was late that afternoon when the flood broke over the small force. William fired till his ammunition was gone, and then he threw rocks. Men died all around him. He felt Sergeant Ambers grab him and pull him away, Louis following. He saw Lieutenant Jones go down, and he knew it was time to run. By 4:30, the last battle line was crumbling and General Hood's army fled in panic toward Franklin.

CHAPTER 23
RETREAT

The woods were full of fleeing men. William, Louis, and Sergeant Ambers stuck together in the darkening forest. William had turned to look back at the edge of the woods, and like Lot's wife, his insides froze. Small bands of desperate Rebels were still fighting, but they were being mowed down like grain before the Federals. Sergeant Ambers drug him by the collar into the woods to safety.

The moon was up high in the cold December night by the time they reached Franklin Pike. "I pray this road is open," Sergeant Ambers gasped as they joined the throng of retreating men shuffling south toward Franklin and the safety of the river.

"If that Yankee cavalry cuts this road, it'll mean a prison camp up north for us," Sergeant Ambers said. "A winter in those awful camps for Southern folks like us is deadly. Getting' home is our best chance of survival."

Confusion and rumors ran up and down the mob of retreating men. A few miles down the Pike, a group of horsemen rode from the woods toward the road. Many men scattered, but several stood and fired into the darkness. Sergeant Ambers pushed the boys off the road, and they crouched in the grass.

"We're Forrest's Cavalry!" came a cry from one of the wounded troopers. The Confederates had fired on their own men trying to join the exodus. The scattered men shuffled back onto the road and continued their flight, hardly noticing the dead men, former comrades who now lay by the road.

William's heart sank to see them come to this. Lieutenant Jones was dead. He was sure of that. He hadn't seen Corporal Heck fall, but he must be dead too. No one could have survived that last fight. He looked at Louis and Sergeant Ambers and their presence helped keep him moving.

William was alone, however, in his thoughts as they moved along. No one spoke in the whole mass of men, each lost in the sadness that comes when your world collapses. How terrible it must be, William thought, for those men whose homes were in Nashville, to have been so close, and now driven away. Where would they run to?

Firing behind them kept them on edge. The shots were close at first, but as the night wore on, it became more and more distant. Still, the men were all fearful that the Federals would come sweeping down on them, or worse yet, would be formed up just over the next rise blocking their escape.

The sun began to rise the next morning, and it shown on a desperate group of men. William found himself in a staggering, shuffling throng. None of their former organization remained. Companies and regiments had ceased to exist. They were now just a mob. Even the officers and sergeants who once yielded so much control over these men's lives were just weary soldiers staggering to an unknown end.

By the time they came to the top of the rise overlooking the Harpeth River and the little town of Franklin, the sun was high in the sky. Men who had fought all day and walked all night began to collapse at the sight of the bridges. It was like they had seen their salvation in front of them and could not make it over. They simply gave out.

As William started down the hill towards the town, two officers rode by, their uniforms torn and their horses staggering. They were talking, and for some reason, William began to listen. "I still can hardly believe it," one said. "Yesterday morning I had a regiment and by sundown, I barely had a platoon, and where they are now, only God knows. I think I'll always remember December 16th as the blackest day of the war." For some reason, that caused a spark in William's exhausted brain and he thought to himself: "That would make today December 17th." It was his 15th birthday.

There were some organized units by the bridges, but they made no effort to stop the men's retreat. William noticed a small knot of horsemen on the northern bank, the side away from safety. General Hood sat there, strapped into his saddle, with tears in his eyes. His staff looked forlorn. Gone were the couriers bustling around them, shot down at Franklin and at Nashville. He looked like a tired, beaten old man, even though he was only thirty-three years old. A few men tried to start a cheer as the column passed, but there were few takers.

William led Sergeant Ambers and Louis toward Captain Richardson's house after they crossed the river. They passed collapsed men everywhere, and were almost sleep walking themselves. Every home in town had already been filled with wounded men from the Franklin battle two weeks before, and now they were inundated with the returning debris of the Army of Tennessee.

The wounded A Company men they had left behind at the Richardson's saw them first. Several shouts went up as William and his friends stumbled through the gate and collapsed on the ground under a large oak tree. They were exhausted and could move no more.

"It's Sergeant Ambers and the boys!" the men shouted and hobbled out to greet them. They called for water and blankets and food.

"What's the news?"

"Where's the rest of the boys?"

The questions came fast, but it was all a blur to William. His vision was encircled by a dark cloud from lack of sleep and utter exhaustion. He was cold and hungry, and completely played out. He saw Mattie come onto the porch, supporting Captain Richardson, and then he fainted.

CHAPTER 24

MATTIE

William awoke in paradise. He felt a softness under him, like he was floating on air, and he was warm for the first time in weeks. Being dead wasn't so bad after all. The next second, his stomach growled and he knew he was still alive, but when he opened his eyes, he couldn't see. It took him a few seconds to determine that someone had placed a cool rag over his face. When his fingers pulled it away, it revealed a room with a fireplace and feather bed.

William tried to remember the last time he had lain on a bed of any kind except the ground. Two months? Was that all? It seemed like a lifetime. As his mind tried to determine where exactly he was and how he got here, he heard a soft, feminine voice.

Mattie Richardson sat in a rocking chair beside him.

"How are you, William?" she said with concern in her voice.

"I'm not sure, Miss Richardson," he said. "I thought I had died and gone to heaven, and now I see it's true."

Mattie blushed, but kept watching his face as he struggled to sit up.

"How long have I been asleep?" he asked.

"Only a few hours, I'm afraid," she confessed. "John, I mean, Captain Richardson, says you and the others have to leave at dark if you're going to keep ahead of the Yankee Cavalry. Oh, William, it's all so awful. The whole army has been pouring into town all day, and they are a mess. John says it's the end."

"I'm afraid it is, Mattie. May I call you that, please?" William wanted to speak frankly to her.

"Yes, William. I'd like that," she said.

"I saw it happen right before my eyes. It was terrible. Lieutenant Jones and so many others are gone. Has anyone else made it back?"

"Just a few and they're in terrible shape like you. I wish I had some clothes to give you. Yours are no better than rags. But we've used all of John's for the wounded men left here."

"It's alright, Mattie," William said her name again. He liked the way saying it made him feel normal, like he hadn't been through so much horror. He rose and pulled on the mule hide moccasins he called shoes. His cartridge belt and rifle lay next to the bed, and he pulled those over his shoulder.

"Mattie, when this war is over, I'd like to see you again."

"That would be nice, William," Mattie said and reached for his hand.

"When I've got the farm back together, I'll come back. Hopefully my Pa will be home from this awful war and our lives will back to normal. I've got some powerful makin' up to do to him. That's when I want to see you, when we're normal people again." He looked out the window to the yard full of broken men. "If that's possible," he added.

Captain Richardson was still very weak, but his wounds were healing. He sat with Sergeant Ambers, Louis, and William in his small study.

"You men have only been with us a short time," he said to them, "and I know you were dragooned into this army. The rest of the boys and I signed up for the duration, so we have to try to reorganize and wait for orders. I think the men who are not wounded will head back into Alabama. The wounded, like myself, will become Union prisoners when they arrive, but I hope they'll leave us here."

He motioned to his wound.

"I'm not going to be much of a threat to them for quite some time, and I expect the war will be over by then. General Lee is bottled up around Richmond and Petersburg in Virginia, and the Union Forces under General Sherman seem to own Georgia, so I think the Confederacy's days are short." He said this in a resigned tone of voice. "So many men have been sacrificed in this war. Ending it will be the best thing. We started off in Nashville three years ago with flags flying, but there's hardly anyone left now. That brings me to you three."

He looked sadly at the man and two boys. Captain Richardson took a sheet of paper and pen from his desk and began to write. When he finished, he handed it to Sergeant Ambers.

"Take this pass with you and leave for your homes tonight. I hope that this will get you through any Confederate troops that stop you." he hesitated. "But my advice to you is to avoid anything that looks like an organized unit. They'll probably be drafting anyone that looks like they can fight, even a one-armed sergeant," he smiled gravely as he tried to lighten the mood.

"But be careful. Yankee cavalry will be everywhere, and if you're caught, you'll spend the rest of the winter in a Prisoner of War camp. Who knows when you'll be released? You also have to watch out for bushwhackers out there. They'll be lots of desperate men whose hope is all gone. I doubt they'll try to rob you, since you all three look worse than any beggars I ever saw, and we've got no food to spare here to give you, but whatever you do, don't lose that paper. It's your only hope of not getting hung as deserters if you're caught by the Confederate patrols. With it, you should be safe."

The Captain leaned back, exhausted. The effort had drained him. "William, when this war is over, come back and visit. Someone here has taken a shine to you, and I believe you are going to grow into a fine man."

If William was not so exhausted, he would have beamed. Instead, he mustered one last salute for this man he respected so much. He had told the Captain earlier about First Sergeant Dillard and Lieutenant Jones, and knew many things weighed heavily on Captain Richardson.

"It's been a pleasure serving with you, sir," Sergeant Ambers said, saluting also. "We'll be on our way, and may God preserve you."

When they reached the porch, the sun was low in the sky and twilight was descending. The night was bitterly cold, and the tattered uniforms they wore were no match for the howling wind.

Sergeant Ambers opened the letter and read it to the boys by the fading light:

Headquarters, CO A, 2nd Tennessee Cavalry
Captain John Richardson
Commanding

    Sergeant Ambers, Private Sweeney, and Private Nix are on official business to Fayetteville Tennessee. Please ensure their safe arrival, and provide them with all the comforts you can spare.

Your Obedient Servant,
John Richardson
Captain, CSA

CHAPTER 25
MOONLIGHT

As they left the house, some of the men had wished them well. William liked the men he had met in Company A, and part of him hated leaving like he was, but all the men sensed the war was over for them, and that the next few months were just a period to be survived.

They saw Henry standing by the gate. William reached out his hand to Henry, who took it and shook, but it was Louis spoke first.

"Henry, it looks like after this you're going to be free. I wish you great good luck in getting' back home to your kin. I wish you well." Louis also reached his hand out to Henry and they shook.

At least the wind was at their backs. The moon was high and shown brightly as William and Louis followed Sergeant Ambers through the gloomy night. Their exodus from Franklin had so far been uneventful. Every house they passed seemed full of weary men. No one had challenged them, even though Sergeant Ambers seemed nervous as they passed each group of men beside the road.

Midnight found them well on their way, and an hour later, Sergeant Ambers decided they were far enough outside the lines that they could stop for a short rest. They avoided any place that looked inhabited, so they found a small ravine in some woods off the road that they could build a small fire out of the wind and out of sight.

The boys gathered fallen wood from the ground and Sergeant Ambers started a fire for them. They dipped their cups in a small stream in the gulley, and Sergeant Ambers dropped several cracked acorns in each. They set their cups in the fire to heat the water, and when the water boiled, they wrapped their caps around the handles so they wouldn't burn their hands.

The hot liquid burned its way down William's throat, and even through the bitter taste, he smiled.

"I know we're all dead tired," Sergeant Ambers said to the boys, "but we'll move on some more tonight. Around daybreak, we'll find ourselves another spot like this."

"What do you think happened to everyone else that left Fayettetown with us, Sergeant?" Louis asked.

Sergeant Ambers gave him a pained look. "I don't think it looks good for any of them. They would have all been at least through what we have seen, and maybe worse."

William often thought of the other men and boys that left their homes with them. He agreed with Sergeant Ambers that their chances of survival were not good.

"I sure can't wait to see the farm," William thought aloud, as much to himself as his companions. "Becky and Jim are snuggled under a great big quilt, and in a few hours, Ma will be up making breakfast."

"We're just a few days from there, boys," Sergeant Ambers said quietly. "By this time next year, God willing, the war will have been over for a while and we'll be back to our lives. You'll tell stories about this here adventure one day to your grandchildren." He smiled weakly at William. "Little Jimmy is going to have about a million questions for you. You better be prepared to answer him for hours."

William also smiled at the thought of his little brother. Jim would be so excited to see him. He knew that he would be intensely curious about William's experience. His smiled waned when he thought about the horror of battle. How could he even talk to Jim about what he had witnessed at Franklin and Nashville?

Sergeant Ambers noticed his pained look.

"When you get back, William," he said, "you've got to take it easy what you tell them. When I got back after losing my arm, we had a difficult time adjusting. I'd wake up at night, scared to death. My temper was short, and I was just plain miserable to be with."

He looked sympathetically at the boys.

"Just because we're away from the fighting doesn't mean it won't be in your mind. You've seen some terrible things that are not easily forgotten. Just don't take it out on the people you love."

Sergeant Ambers dashed out the remaining water from his cup on the small fire and gathered his gear.

"Let's get a few more miles toward home," and the three of them crept out of the woods and continued their journey.

CHAPTER 26
SHELTER

The sun came up over the frigid Tennessee landscape, and the wind still howled in from the north, but the day was clear. William, Louis, and Sergeant Ambers had been looking for a place to camp for the last half hour as the night sky lightened ever so slightly. William hoped they would spot a farmhouse safely off the road where they could spend the day in relative warmth.

They had been moving along a fence line about half a mile from the main road. At night, the fence line proved fairly easy to follow, and the fields provided enough separation from the road to keep them obscured. Several times throughout the night, groups of riders could be heard out on the road.

Sergeant Ambers and the boys would crouch behind the fence until the noise faded in the distance. Luckily for them, these units were too small to have outlying riders. As soon as the sun came up, however, it would be harder to hide.

They angled away from the road on a small track heading southeast through a grove of trees. The leafless branches hung gloomily over the trail, and the morning mist billowed softly around William's feet. This area reminded him of the hidden area where he had kept his livestock back at the farm.

William and Louis followed Sergeant Ambers as he moved slowly, watching carefully. Fifty yards in, they spotted on old, decrepit barn in a clearing ahead. As they got closer to it, they stopped and lay in the grass to see if it was occupied. A foraging party from either army, North or South, could be dangerous to them now. They could be captured or shot by Federal troops, as they were still armed Confederates. They could also be captured and returned to the Rebel army retreating to Alabama if the barn was occupied by Confederates, or be shot as deserters if they ran into a Rebel officer who disagreed with the Captain's note.

Anything could happen when an Army disintegrated. Thousands of men who were living under authority suddenly had no one to be responsible to or for. Logistics shut down, so already scarce supplies of food and other essentials virtually ceased to exist. Add to this an army of Federal troops bent on capturing as many Rebels as it could, and chaos reigned.

Sergeant Ambers watched the barn for about 10 minutes before he motioned William to one side and Louis to the other. The boys checked the percussion caps on their rifles to make sure they were loaded, and they moved silently toward the barn, hugging the tree on either side of the clearing. Sergeant Ambers leveled his big pistol at the house for cover.

William could feel his heart pounding in his chest. He scanned his eyes around the clearing in the dawn light, but saw no movement except for Louis. The boys circled the clearing and then ran low up to the sides of the barn. They peered through the gaps between the board walls, but it was still too dark to see inside.

Sergeant Ambers rose and walked toward them out of the mist. His pistol would be much more effective in case they ran into trouble in the barn.

Flanked by the boys, rifles at the ready, Sergeant Ambers quietly pushed in the barn door, fully expecting the blast of a shotgun aimed at him any second.

"Good so far," he thought as the door cracked open. He could see some of the inside in the gloom, and he was still alive.

"Let's go, boys, all at once and real quiet." The three of them pushed their way in, guns leveled.

Nothing.

The empty barn stood before them like an inviting mansion. The musty old piles of straw on the floor and the instant absence of the biting wind settled their jangled nerves almost immediately.

William and Louis searched the barn for anything usable, while Sergeant Ambers secured the door.

"They've got a cellar under here," Louis reported back. "Good work, Louis," Sergeant Ambers called. "You boys check it out and make sure there's no rattlers snuggled in there for the winter, and we'll cover it over real good and sleep there. We're only a day away from Franklin and there's a good chance this barn'l be passed by someone.'

William took a match from Sergeant Ambers and lit a stub of candle he carried. Louis opened the cellar door, and William, candle in one hand and Sergeant Ambers' pistol in the other, jumped down into the blackness of the cellar.

It did not take his eyes long to get used to the darkness. The cellar wasn't big, maybe ten feet by ten feet, and he had to crouch under the beams of the barn floor over his head. He searched all around with his small candle and it looked totally empty.

"Looks good down here," he said as he popped his head back up. Standing, his head and shoulders cleared the floor.

"Let's get our gear down there quick and settle in. Louis, grab that empty crate over there so I've got something to stand on to climb out. With only one arm, I'd have a devil of a time getting' out of there," he smiled at the boys. "We're going to have a good sleep today, boys!"

They disturbed as little as possible in the barn, and did their best to make it look like no one had been there. Sergeant Ambers lowered himself down and the boys covered the trap door with as much as straw and junk they could find to camouflage it. Louis slid down, and as William closed the door over his head, he did his best to brush straw over the crack in the opening.

It was much warmer in the cellar, though still cold. They wrapped up in their blankets and huddled together for warmth. Sergeant Ambers knew that they should take turns on watch in case a patrol came through, but he was so tired by this time, he just closed his eyes and went to sleep, quickly followed by two exhausted boys.

CHAPTER 27
A SURPRISE

Clomp, Clomp, Clomp. Heavy boots over their heads woke all three with a start. They dared not move. They hardly let out a breath.

Clomp, Clomp, Clomp, then silence. Some low voices outside. The sound of jingling horse harnesses.

"Anything in there, O'Malley?" a voice called from outside. Williams's eyes met Louis', and then flicked in the darkness to Sergeant Ambers. William thought that voice outside sounded Southern. "Looks empty, Sarge," the man standing right over their heads replied. His accent was heavily laden with Irish brogue, making it impossible to tell which Army he belonged to. Irishmen fought for both sides. Even their own General Cleburne, who died at Franklin, was Irish.

Clomp, Clomp. More men entered. There appeared to be two or three men inside the barn. Their heavy boots told Sergeant Ambers they were probably cavalrymen, and by the sound of them he guessed they were Federal since most southerner's boots were so worn out by now, he guessed they'd make a softer sound.

No matter. They had to remain hidden no matter what. He had to get these two boys home. Sergeant Ambers looked at the boys rolled in their blankets, their eyes wide with fright.

"Relax," he mouthed to them. "Just be quiet." He knew that was easier said than done. They all hoped their camouflage job on the cellar door would continue hiding them.

We'll camp here tonight, men," they heard the southern voice call out. "Let's go get the horses tied up away from the wind. Corporal Jessup, your squad's on picket tonight. Keep your men alert. We're deep down past Franklin and the Rebs might move this way heading east."

Williams's heart sank. He thought he would become ill right then and there. These men were Federals!

Sergeant Ambers had the same thought. Could the three of them remain hidden all night right under the nose of an entire Yankee cavalry patrol sleeping above them? He knew if they were caught, it would be a northern prison for them. He knew the awful reality of that: disease, starvation, and months of boredom waiting for the war to end. Many died, forgotten and lonely in those northern camps.

The barn was full of men now. William could hear bedrolls and saddles dropping on the floor above their heads, and lots of low voices. He could hear the sounds of horses tied to the barn outside. It was pitch dark in the cellar, so he assumed they had slept all day and this was a Yankee patrol putting up here for the night to get out of the cold. It was excruciating to lay completely still, frozen in terror.

Two men dropped their saddles and arranged their bedrolls right above them. One of them appeared to be the sergeant with the southern twang to his voice. Several times men came up to the sergeant to ask for instructions. Somehow, William found his voice comforting, despite the terror of his predicament. His voice, though muffled, sounded kind and somewhat familiar.

As the Federal soldiers settled in, snores began to fill the barn. The two men above the cellar left for awhile; presumably, William decided, to check on their pickets. When they returned, William heard them sit above them and pull off their boots. A light flickered above them, and the faint smell of tobacco smoke filled the air.

"This has been one hell of a couple of days," the Sergeant said. "It feels good to be back in Tennessee. You ever been here, O'Malley?" the Yankee sergeant asked.

"No, Sarge," the man named O'Malley answered. "I came west from New York to Indiana and then to St. Louis. When we formed up with you in St, Louis, that's the farthest south I'd been."

"Well, I'll tell you, O'Malley, it's good to be back in Tennessee. I left here two years ago, and the Army's had me in Missouri fighting in the back country since then. This is the closest I've been to home in a long time.

Williams's heart skipped a beat. He knew Sergeant Ambers and Louis were listening to this conversation also. That voice.....

"I haven't heard from my family in two years," the Sergeant continued. "I've got a farm south of here, a lovely wife and three kids. When they moved our Regiment from Missouri to Tennessee by steamboat last week that was about the best news I've ever heard."

"What're your children's names, Sarge?" O'Malley asked.

"Jim's my youngest; he's a little spit fire. Then there's Becky, my girl, and William, my oldest, is probably a man now."

"PA!" William's voice shot through the air like a rifle bullet! The two Yankees leapt to their feet, and William heard pistols draw from their holsters.

Sergeant Ambers, lying next to William froze even stiffer than before.

"Pa! It's William! Don't shoot, Pa! I'm down here in the cellar with Louis and Mr. Ambers!' Williams's voice cracked with the tension and excitement.

"Come out of there, you!" The Yankee Sergeant yelled. Other voices were audible now, as the whole barn of men began to come alive. "Hands up, let me see 'em!"

William heard the cock of several pistols.

"Dear, God, William," Sergeant Ambers hissed, "We're going to die. It's dark in here, so you raise up real slow and keep your hands high!"

"Mr. Sweeney, I pray that's you, sir," Mr. Ambers' voice rose through the floor. "This is John Ambers. This here is your boy, William. He's raising up through the floor, so for God's sake, don't let anybody blow his head off!"

"Hold your fire, men! Nobody shoot!" The Yankee Sergeant called loudly. "William, or whoever you are, come out real slow."

William wanted to leap through the door. He knew that was his Pa's voice up there, but he was terrified at the same time. Very carefully, he sat up.

"I'm coming up, Pa." Tears began streaming down his face. Two years of emotion and a lifetime of fear began to pour from him. His hands pushed open the door, and slowly, his head emerged from the floor. A small lantern had been lit in the barn, and he had just enough light to look down the barrel of a big pistol.

"William! By God, it is you!" His father shouted. "Put down your guns, boys! We've got us a miracle here!"

He reached down and hauled William out of the cellar. Father embraced son for the first time in two years, while men in blue and gray looked on in disbelief.

CHAPTER 28
FACE TO FACE WITH THE GENERAL

Big warm blankets were produced and wrapped around the shoulders of the boys and Sergeant Ambers. Huge grins were visible in the lantern light as Sergeant Ambers detailed their journey. William huddled under the big arm of his father. He kept looking at him to make sure he wasn't dreaming.

"Pa," William said at last, "we didn't know if you were even alive. We've gotten no letters since you left!" "I've been sending them, William, but they must not have made it past the lines. They sent me right away to Missouri, and I've been fighting there for two years. It's an awful business out there, mostly fighting bushwhackers and guerrillas."

"How's your Ma and Becky and Jim? When did you see them last?" Pa asked.

William told his Pa about the day the riders came to the cabin and took him to the army. He told him about the camp and the march to Franklin. His voice cracked more than once as he described his ordeals of the past weeks.

"It's alright now, William," his Pa said time and time again. "We'll get you home somehow. This war out here has got to be almost over."

"I didn't do very well takin' care of the farm Pa," William admitted, expecting the wrath he had been used to two years back. "I let the mule get stole because I was careless. I should have listened to you more and paid more attention to the lessons you were teachin' me."

"Don't you fret about any of that now William," John Sweeney said. "I've learned a lot out here, too, and I'm a different man than I was back home. I've learned not to dwell on the small things in life. More than once, as we've ridden by farms in Missouri, I would have traded anything to be back at the farm with you and the family. We'll start over and I'll treat you more like a man. With all you've seen, you deserve as much."

"Pa," William said, his tone hushed so no one around them could here, "right now I just want to be your little boy. I'm tired of trying to be a grown up."

They talked long through the night. Sergeant Ambers and William's father discussed their options and decided that the best course of action would be to take the three Confederates back to the Federal colonel in charge of Sergeant Sweeney's regiment. Everyone sensed the war was coming to a close, and perhaps they could find a way to get the boys and Sergeant Ambers back home, or at least keep them safe until the war ended. John Sweeney was especially worried about his wife and two small children back on his farm.

The next morning William swung up into the saddle behind his father. Louis and Sergeant Ambers did the same with two other troopers. William had never felt so good as when he held on tightly to his Pa on this ride back to the Federal camp.

By late morning they arrived at the field headquarters of the Federal cavalry regiment. John Sweeney rode his little detachment right up to the colonel's tent. He got strange looks as he dismounted with a young Confederate private in tow. William did his best to look like a man, and walked beside his father toward the colonel's tent with his head held high. One of the sentries called inside for the colonel.

"What do we have here?" the Yankee officer asked Sergeant Sweeney as he stepped from the tent. "Rebel prisoners? Take them over to the Provost Marshall to be shipped up north!"

Sergeant Sweeney saluted, and then grinned at the colonel. "I just can't do that sir. You see, this is my son, William, and our two friends. We found them last night trying to make their way back home."

The colonel stared in disbelief. As the story unfolded, William realized the officer was a good-natured man who appreciated the uniqueness of the situation. "That's the goll-darndest thing I've ever heard of Sergeant." He turned to his orderly, "Let's get this boy and his friends some hot food. They're never going to believe this back in Nashville."

The Federal regiment had patrol duty, but the colonel agreed that William and Louis and Mr. Ambers could travel along with them until they could circle back to their base. It was five days before they came in sight of Nashville again, and by then their "prisoners" had become more like mascots.

It was late in the afternoon when William, Louis, and Sergeant Ambers, disarmed of course, trotted borrowed horses along side the colonel, Sergeant Sweeney, and the Yankee patrol into Nashville to General George Thomas' headquarters, and William saw first-hand the power of the Federal army. Nashville was full of soldiers, cannon, horses, and supplies, even though many of the Federal troops were off in pursuit of General Hood's shattered army. William rode beside his father and as they crossed the battlefield, he told his Pa and the colonel of his part in the battle.

When they reached General Thomas' headquarters, the colonel went in and had a short conversation with one of the staff officers. Through the window, William could see him gesture outside several times, and the look of disbelief was clear on the other man's face. The staff officer walked back in to another room for a few minutes. When he returned he ushered William and his father inside.

Sergeant Sweeney snapped to attention, as did William, when they entered General Thomas's office. The general returned the salute and then walked from behind his desk and shook Sergeant Sweeney's hand, then slapped William on the back. "This is the best story I've heard all day, Sergeant!" the general boomed. "It's about time I heard some happy news. In all of this death and trouble, it's time good fortune smiled on someone in this terrible war. Tell me how this came about."

Sergeant Sweeney retold the story of finding William, and General Thomas beamed.

"Call the colonel in," General Thomas said to his orderly after John had finished. When Sergeant Sweeney's commander returned, General Thomas gave him an order: "Send a strong patrol with Sergeant Sweeney and his son and friends with a flag of truce down to Fayetteville and let's reunite this family. This war is almost over and we need to be making some gestures of reconciliation. We're all Americans and we'll need to live together in peace when this bloody mess is over."

The general looked at William. "Some day you'll look back on all this and be grateful for the divine hand of Providence in your deliverance. Raise your right hand, William, and swear you'll never again take up arms against the Union."

William raised his hand, swore his oath, and became a citizen of the United States again. Louis and Mr. Ambers were then brought in and they did the same.

General Thomas reached in his pocket and pulled out several crumpled dollars. "Sergeant Sweeney, go buy this boy some civilian clothes and some new shoes to keep him warm. God bless you both and Merry Christmas!"

Neither William nor his father had realized that this was December 24, 1864.

CHAPTER 29
BUSHWHACKERS

The next morning William joined a small patrol of Federal cavalry and headed toward home. He and his friends rode borrowed horses and trotted in the middle of the formation behind his father and his squad of troopers. William had on a new pair of trousers and a shirt, a pair of socks and sturdy cavalry boots, an overcoat, a wool cap, and a warm scarf. Louis and Mr. Ambers also had some new warm clothes, mostly donated by the United States cavalry.

A Union captain rode at the head of the patrol, and William felt safe among this heavily armed body of men. Compared to the Confederates he had been with, these men looked well fed, well mounted and armed to the teeth.

They traveled all day and camped by a small creek for the evening. William watched the pickets and sentries take their positions, and he enjoyed watching the easy manner in which his father commanded his men. He could see that his father had mellowed, and that he obviously had earned his sergeant stripes.

William bedded down next to his father, and Mr. Ambers and Louis lay down close beside them. It was a quiet, moonless night, and William drifted off to sleep with the sounds of the horses breathing on their own picket rope just a few feet away.

About midnight William woke. He was not sure what had startled him, so he lay still and listened intently to the night sounds. All was quiet, and pretty soon he decided to chance the cold air and walk out to the bushes and relieve his bladder. He was extra careful not to wake anyone.

He had gone about ten paces outside of the camp when he heard something again. It sounded like footsteps in the brush, moving very slowly. He peered through the night but saw nothing. He held his breath and felt his heart pounding in his chest.

A thud and a muffled cry came from the darkness. It sounded to William like the noise a hog makes when you knock him in the head before slaughter. As William turned to break for the camp, a rush of men came out of the darkness just beside him, running for the horses. They must not have seen him, and he crouched for an instant before the first blast of a pistol, and then another came from the rushing men. William heard the sleeping men in the Federal camp begin to curse and fumble for their weapons. There was more firing now, and William sensed the marauders were making a run for the horses.

"Bushwhackers! Bushwhackers!" William began to yell to the camp as loud as he could. He knew if he ran toward the camp he might get shot down by either side in the confusion, but the thought of his father out there needing warning overcame his fear. He bolted toward his Pa.

"William! William!" He heard his father shouting over the din. He must have discovered William was missing.

"Here Pa, I'm coming!" William yelled back. He saw his father through the gloom running towards him. A figure stepped from the darkness and aimed a pistol in his Pa's direction, and William swerved toward him, just in time to knock the gun up and away as it fired. He looked into the face of a wild eyed man for just an instant, before the butt of the pistol cracked down on William's skull. William spun to the ground. He felt, rather than saw, a figure crash out of the darkness and lunge at his assailant, knocking him aside. As William lost consciousness he knew his Pa stood over him, protecting him.

CHAPTER 30

HOME

William, his father, Mr. Ambers, and Louis rode into Fayetteville two days later. William carried a slash across his forehead, and it hurt to the touch, but he was okay. His father was unhurt, and the little column of Federal troopers they rode with still had every man. The bushwhackers had all run off and escaped before they could be taken prisoner, except for the man John Sweeney had killed defending William. One sentry, the one William heard out in the bushes, also sported a bandage wrapped around his head from the fight.

They pulled up at Mr. Ambers' house. William and Louis dismounted with the one-armed man and hugged him tightly.

"Thank you, Mr. Ambers," William said, tears in his eyes. "I'll come see you soon." William's father shook hands with Mr. Ambers and thanked him for looking after William.

"John," Mr. Ambers said to William's father, "You've got a mighty fine boy there. He served well and did his duty, and I hope everything's okay back at your farm. I'm sorry to have been the one to drag him off into all this, but thank goodness he's home safe. I can sleep easy now. Please forgive me for getting him caught up in this war."

He turned to William. "You're a brave lad, William. Be good to your brother and sister. They'll want to know everything, and you partial out to them what you think is right. You've seen the elephant and lived to tell about, and let's hope they never have to do the same. You come see me if you need to talk."

Mr. Ambers' wife rushed out and, looking perplexed at the Federal troops, ushered her husband inside.

The trip to the Nix farm was brief and filled with emotion for William and his friend. They dropped off Louis at his farm and watched the excited homecoming there. Louis and William shook hands like men before William rode away.

As the Sweeney gate came into view, William looked at his father and thought of the many miles and great strife that lay behind them. He saw tears well in his father's eyes at these thoughts too.

The Union captain pulled up the little column at the gate. He, William, and Sergeant Sweeney dismounted. The captain reached into his dispatch case and produced a sheaf of papers.

"Sergeant Sweeney, you've served your country well for two years in some terrible fighting in Missouri and now you've been reunited with your son through a miracle. You've given us all a ray of hope that some day soon we'll all get back to our own families."

"Thank you, Sir," Sergeant Sweeney said, surprised at the unexpected praise. He looked over the captain's shoulder at the home he had not seen in two years and put his hand on William's shoulder.

"General Thomas drafted this letter for you before we left his headquarters," the captain continued, and he held it up to read:

Headquarters
Department of Tennessee
Nashville, Tennessee
To whom it may concern,
    The bearer of this letter, Sergeant John Sweeney, after two years of valorous service to the Army of the United

States of America, is ordered discharged this 24th day of December, 1864, with the sincere thanks of the nation, and is hereby authorized to return to his home to live a peaceful and fruitful life."

George H. Thomas
Major General, U S Army
Commanding

John Sweeney, now a civilian, stared at his officer in stunned disbelief. He and William were coming home to stay! When they walked through that gate, neither would have to serve in this war again. He saluted his captain, shook the hands of the men he had served with for so long, and wrapped his arm around William for the walk up to the house.

"Keep the horses, John," the captain added, "as a gift from a grateful nation. You'll need them for the spring planting."

William unhooked the clasp from the gate, and he and his father led their horses through. Ida Sweeney, followed by Becky and Jim, ran from the house when they recognized them. William Sweeney put his arm around his father, and they walked up the lane toward home, each with newfound respect for the other.

EPILOGUE

The Civil War ended four months later and hundreds of thousands of soldiers in blue and gray returned home. Ahead was the task of rebuilding their shattered country.

John and Ida Sweeney returned to their life on the farm with their children, but William continued to dream of his future. That summer, after the new crops were in, he rode to Franklin to see his old captain who was still recovering from his wounds – and he also went to see Mattie, who continued to stay in his thoughts.

William hoped the next chapter of his life would be one of peace and happiness, but he never forgot his comrades and friends from that terrible Confederate winter of 1864.

AUTHOR'S NOTE

William Sweeney was a real person, and was my great, great, great grandfather. At 14 he was drafted into the Confederate Army for the last great battles in the Western Theater. The historical details in this book are as accurate as I and my co-author could make them, but William's regiment, the 2nd Tennessee Cavalry (Dismounted), is a fictitious unit, not to be confused with the real Confederate 2nd Tennessee Cavalry (of which there appears to have been four) which fought honorably throughout the war. General Daniel Govan's brigade, General Patrick Cleburne's Division, General Frank Cheatham's Corps, and General John Bell Hood's Army of Tennessee were all real, however, as depicted here. The accounts of the battles of Spring Hill, Franklin, and Nashville, are accurately portrayed in all their horror, confusion, and heroism, although the two days at Nashville are compressed into one. Of course, there were a few times when the truth had to be "fudged" a little, or the time frame compressed for the good of the story.

William's journeys and most of the characters he meets along the way are from my imagination, but his participation in these events is a matter of public record in the archives of the Civil War. These dramatic events helped shape his life and the lives of every generation of Americans that has followed him.